BETTER ENDINGS

A Guidebook for Creative Re-visioning

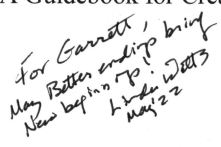

For Garrett,
May Better endings bring
New beginning! Linda Watts
May '22

Linda K. Watts

CENTRAL PARK SOUTH PUBLISHING

BETTER ENDINGS

Published by Central Park South Publishing 2022
www.centralparksouthpublishing.com

Cover design by Estella Vukovic
Typesetting and e-book formatting by Victor Marcos

ISBN:
Paperback: 978-1-956452-08-2
Hardback: 978-1-956452-09-9
eBook: 978-1-956452-10-5

Acknowledgements

I dedicate this book to Sophie and Emily Watts, whose loving energy underscores the entirety of its message. I am grateful also to the following two-legged critters for their emotional, intellectual, and spiritual guidance and support: Janet Parker, Rev. Lee Ireland, Susan Plumb, Linda Langton, Cheryl Watts, Carole Poulter, Keith and Judy Watts, Anne and Karis Lyon, Kathleen and Tatyana Ulrich, Barb and Neal Carman, Pam Flynn, Jan Jerrold, Arlene and Darlene Peina, Denise Naughton, PJ Arriza, Diane and Michael McNally, Polly Nelson, Geralyn Felicetta, Dr. Herbert Richardson, UCCS and Ithaca College Anthropology faculty and students; and Sri Harold Klemp.

Contents

PART ONE

The Art of Better Endings

Introduction

Several years ago I walked out of a movie theatre at the point that King Kong, in the Peter Jackson version of this epic tale, was about to tumble into his fatal fall from the top of the Empire State Building. 'Not again!' I told myself; I did not relish witnessing yet another rendition of the Great Kong's demise.

I slipped out of the theatre and went to a local cafe where I took out pen and notebook and composed what was for me a more satisfying 'better ending' scenario for the classic *King Kong* tale.

In my re-visioned story, Kong lives! I will share my new ending for this tale in the next chapter. For now, let me share that the very act of changing this iconic storyline felt liberating. I felt empowered by the creative license I had assumed.

I started thinking about other movies and fictional stories with endings I had always disliked. Wouldn't it be fun to twist these endings, too?

Over the next few months, I wrote several fictional "better endings" scenarios. Finally, in my re-visioning, Juliet awakens just in time to stop her beloved Romeo from imbibing his vial of poison, and their marriage after such resolve leads to an improvement of relations for the feuding Montagues and Capulets, altering European history from the prodigy of these star-crossed lovers ever since! The battered Jack Twist of *Brokeback Mountain* survives his brutal homophobic attack and the gallant couple of Ennis and Jack move to Wyoming together to start a llama ranch near a commune with inspiring, open-minded Sufi neighbors. Eventually Ennis and Jack marry, and Ennis's daughter who lives with them mentors Sufi children, who together later make a substantial contribution to climate change-related sustainable ranching.

In my re-visioned story endings, women in the final scenes of a whole slew of novels and movies (e.g., the Helen Hunt character in *What Women Want*) choose to NOT quit their jobs to relocate or otherwise diminish their own life potentials in support of their husbands' privileged ambitions. African American protagonists get to live and thrive without grieving their family members from brutal street gang or police violence. In these (for me) *better endings*, creative, goal-seeking characters fulfill their life dreams without being unduly restrained by systemic prejudice or discrimination.

After a while I realized I could re-vision not only fictional outcomes but also historical events. What if Abraham Lincoln had survived his gunshot wound or Martin Luther King, Jr. and J.F.K. had survived their assassination attempts and gone on to institute progressive cultural change? As with time travel generally, such radical changes of historical moments would have deep and expansive implications for where we might all be today. "Where were you when Kennedy survived?" could have become a more significant meme than where you were when he died.

I established a first principle for my historical reconstructions: I could only alter history by transforming it with life-affirming, positive twists. I would not allow myself to conceptually birth a Hitler whose Third Reich won World War II, for instance; that felt like a healthy rule to impose.

I found that with every *better ending* narrative fabric I re-wove, I felt better too! It was empowering, liberating to contemplate positive, alternative potentials unwinding from these revisionist fictional and historical threads.

Eventually as I continued with my *better endings* writing practice, I realized how this freed me to re-vision my own past, present and future! This is where I ventured next. Significant decisions and choices I have made, relationships I have entered into or ended, big moves I have made, goals I have set, even significant nightly dreams that had left me feeling unsettled or fearful; all of these were ripe for creative re-visioning by applying what I now understand as the natural, constructive principle of Better Endings.

This book offers opportunities for you to practice applying the creative principle of Better Endings for yourself; to explore and reflect about personally meaningful fictional stories and historical events as well as your own significant life experiences and goals. Each chapter introduces a topical theme that is ripe for exploring *better endings*. I will provide sample stories and reflections based on my own or others' life experiences to model the technique, then a section with Better Endings Story Seed journaling prompts along with lined starter-journaling pages at the end of each chapter guide you to develop your own *better endings* stories around the chapter's theme.

Please establish for yourself a dedicated, separate Better Endings Journal where you can engage freely—beyond or in addition to the starter journaling pages provided—with the chapter-ending Better Endings Story Seed prompts, to compose and compile your own *better endings* revisionist ideas. In your Better Endings Journal sandbox, you can play with the chapter themes without space restrictions, writing one or perhaps several 'alternate' story lines about one or more of the topics you will be invited to list as you explore and gain personal insights.

Please understand from the start of your adventure in better-endering that the sort of alternate story conclusions I am inviting you to imagine are not necessarily "happy endings," nor am I asking you to employ merely pie-in-the-sky, wishful or magical thinking. I do not think it is to anyone's greatest value to use the Better Endings tool as a Happily Ever After romantic fantasy device so they can avoid or deny hard facts. Rather, I encourage you to exercise and learn to flex your creative re-visioning muscles so that you might forge real *better endings* with your life choices going forward.

So, rather than 'happily ever-aftering' as in fairytale magical thinking, better-endering (or, better rendering) empowers you to develop creative visualization and planning skills so you can self-actualize *better endings* in your own life.

For example, one of my favorite movies whose ending I initially found unsatisfying (but always ask yourself, why? when you find yourself having a gut reaction to a movie's ending) is *Castaway*. I wanted Chuck Noland and Kelly Frears to marry and live happily-ever-after family lives after Chuck has survived his horrendous five-year ordeal on a remote tropical island. Why couldn't Kelly have finished her Ph.D. and waited for Chuck to return, as in the story's opening he had clearly promised her he would?

After several viewings of this film *Castaway* with which I can personally identify, I have come to see how the ending is, even for me, an appropriate conclusion. Chuck's ordeals on the island and his resolve to return to Kelly have altered him; he cannot go back to being the person he was when he was with Kelly, and she must go forward from the state of consciousness she has attained from processing her loss. This transformational tale has a bittersweet ending as both protagonists find their paths winding forward again; new potentials have unfolded for all!

Part One topics in this book will invite you to engage with fictional and historical re-visioning. Part Two journaling prompts will guide you to apply the principle of Better Endings to creatively re-vision pivotal events and situations from your own life story: past, present, and future.

Applying the creative principle of Better Endings to your own life experiences and goals can empower you to strengthen your capacity to see, be, and act as you consciously choose rather than as you might have felt compelled to accept before reclaiming your virtually unlimited, innate "creative license."

You are the author, editor, and the heroic protagonist of your own life story. May you learn here how to script your own *better endings*!

When I first conceived of writing this book, I imagined the title as it appears on the front cover right away: let's focus not on *bItter*, but rather on *bEtter* endings! I suppose this penchant to look for silver linings and to encourage transformative, positive change comes from my own naturally optimistic outlook on life. The glass is always a bit more than half full even if we might need to tilt the cup in our direction sometimes, right? In my first childhood role on stage for a second-grade play, I was cast as an elderly British lady wearing "rose colored glasses," and as I remember the story, her optimism was helpfully contagious!

Yet there is far more than cockeyed optimism available to you here. I believe in Better Endings! I believe what you conceive of you CAN manifest, so why focus on anything less than the realization of your most worthy goals? By the way, age does not matter, at all! No matter how old or how young you are, and regardless of how happy or sad you might be feeling, you can benefit from practicing the art of *better endings*.

Let's consider first, then, what this creative principle of Better Endings is about, which you can use to steer your life—despite your stickiest memories or questionable choices—toward more beneficial outcomes and conditions.

The principle or faculty of Better Endings is dynamic, constructive, and practical as well as being inherently flexible and creative. It can help you develop your innate and many would say your divine gift of imagination which is built into your adaptive survival toolkit as a human being. Your creative imagination is what allows you to anticipate possible and probable future consequences of your actions and to reflect upon decisions, actions or attitudes from the past that have brought you to where you are today. Focussing on Better Endings as a creative tool allows you to envision and bring about your most desirable future conditions and lets you contemplate what could—with slight revisions of choice—have led to more optimal outcomes from your past.

So, let's get started. I have organized the topical themes in this book to mirror my own gradual process in developing the art of *better ending* creative re-visioning. Part One journaling prompts invite you to playfully imagine new endings for popular stories and historical moments; then Part Two journaling prompts guide you to creatively re-vision some of your own life events and to envision practical pathways to fulfill your most desirable future.

It is normal to feel some initial resistance to applying the principle of Better Endings to your own life experiences. When I ask people what they might have done differently regarding significant turning points in their life, they often respond 'Nothing,' even when things may not have worked out optimally from some of their past choices. We might tell ourselves:

How dare you tamper with Reality as it is written in stone? Isn't life all about adjusting to inevitabilities that eventually form a hardened crust around your daily routines—or, around your heart? What's life without a touch of bitterness, after all? No pain, no gain, right? After all, you would not be where you are today if your life had not unfolded exactly as it has!

Accepting "bittersweet" yesteryear decisions that have turned out as well or better than we might have hoped for is fine, of course; especially if we have managed to squeeze out from our past lemons some meaningful life lesson 'juice.' Still, there is always an advantage to reviewing the past if we wish to move forward with mindful awareness.

It is also interesting to recognize from the start how the principle of Better Endings is so deeply embedded in language. We speak metaphorically of finding silver linings in hardship, of passing through a meaningful darkness before the dawn, or of making lemonade from lemons; so, applying the principle of Better Endings is a natural human capacity. Use it or lose it!

With each of the chapters in this book, I will introduce a theme and share examples usually from my own forays into creative re-visioning around that theme. Then I will turn the topic over to you. Better Endings Story Seed journaling prompts will guide you to imagine and compose your own *better endings* scenarios around the chapter's theme, in the lined pages provided, or further in your Better Endings Journal. You will find the Better Endings Story Seed journaling prompts at the end of every chapter below the Acorn icon. The Acorn matures to become the mighty Oak, fulfilling its innate *better endings* potential!

You can record your own lists of topics or events from your life to explore by writing these lists directly in the open spaces provided in the Better Endings Story Seed sections. Then please use the starter pages provided and/or your separate, private Better Endings Journal— of whatever size or blank-page book format you choose—to explore the chapters' topics and creatively compose your personal *better endings* stories. After composing one or more of your own story ideas, the Story Seed prompts will encourage you to also journal about your personal reflections in a *My Reflections* section for each chapter theme in the starter pages provided or in your separate Better Endings Journal. Here you can reflect freely about your insights and life lessons gleaned from your creative practice of imagining *better endings*.

Are you ready to reclaim your creative capacity to re-vision fiction and history and to apply the principle of Better Endings to your own life story? Well then, and let's go!

Better Endings Story Seed

Introduction to Part One: The Art of Better Endings

1. You may use the blank lined pages following the Better Endings Story Seed chapter-ending sections in this book as journaling spaces. You may also wish to establish your own separate Better Endings Journal for journaling more extensively, beyond the 'starter' journal pages provided. Use the journaling pages provided and/or your own Better Endings Journal for exploring the themes in this book by composing your own *better endings* stories in response to the journaling prompts in the chapter-ending Better Endings Story Seed sections throughout this book.

2. After you have responded to the Story Seed prompts in the journal pages provided and/or in your Better Endings Journal for a chapter, be sure to add your personal reflections and insights You may use the My Reflections journaling section provided after each chapter's blank journaling pages, and/or your own Better Endings Journal..

3. As you embark on your self-discovery journey with this book, how do you relate to the basic idea of Better Endings? What are *better endings*, to you? You may use the space below to begin your journaling process, and/or use your Better Endings Journal directly.

Chapter 1

From Bitter to Better Endings: At the Movies

M ovies are a natural starting place for putting the principle of
Better Endings into practice. I have sometimes wished the film
industry would offer viewers a set of available alternate endings for its
movies. Then you could select which ending you would prefer to watch,
or try out several! Movies provide us with a grand projective device,
a way to see our own passions or true-life dramas exteriorized on
the big screen. So, it would only make sense for there to be alternate
endings to better suit different demographic groups of viewers.
Yet given the added expense that would bring to film production
along with the fact that authors and screenwriters would find it
cumbersome to have to tailor their artistic vision to a wide range of
viewers, we are left with the creative license offered with this book,
to compose our very own 'better endings.'

Please keep in mind as you select a film and contemplate a new
twist to its conclusion that you are crafting YOUR vision for what
could happen, were this your story to tell. This creative re-visioning
practice is similar to dream interpretation: what would someone else's

dream mean to you if it were your dream? Of course, the film script or someone else's dream remains sacrosanct as their own, but when they share it with you it is only natural for you to project yourself into the story.

We naturally make a story our own whenever we watch a movie or read a book or listen to someone else's dream. It can be useful to consider how you would modify a film so it is more relevant to your experience or more satisfying to you. How would YOU wish that a particular movie could end? Why do you prefer this different ending? What does your *better ending* version reveal about you; does it relate to situations or experiences from your own life that you might also wish to change or tweak in keeping with your inherent creative license? An underlying sub-theme throughout this book is 'Change a story, change a life': yours!

So, let's try this on:

KONG LIVES!

Kong's fateful fall from the Empire State Building still takes place in my re-telling of this monumental tale, but with the heroine still cradled firmly in one gargantuan hand, the Great Kong breaks his fall twice on the way down to the ground from sheer willpower, clutching desperately at the side of the building to slow his descent out of his super-primate love for Ann Darrow and a primal unwillingness to let her die. At the base of the building where Kong has landed with his beloved still cushioned in his palm, he is injured by the impact, but he and she have both survived. Still from his primate instinct to protect Ann from the dark forces of urban inhumanity, Kong drags himself away from the building as the military stalls from closing in. They and a large gathering of bystanders have assumed Kong could not have survived the fall, so they have rallied around at the front side of the building for a quick press conference and to organize how to haul away Kong's carcass.

Kong limps with Ann now unconscious in his hand, instinctively navigating through mostly empty late-night alleyways back to the frozen lake in Central Park where she and he had communed, in the Jackson film version, just before their would-have-been fateful climb up the Empire State building.

Ann awakens as they reach Central Park and surveys the situation. She leads Kong deep into a little known, trail-less, woodsy region she knows of in the park. There they lay low while Ann uses a powerful backstage theater prop walkie-talkie that for protective reasons Jack Driscoll had slipped into her pocket (remember, it is 1933). Ann calls Jack, the screenwriter —still in my version played by Adrien Brody— who is also smitten with her. Given this chance to finally win Ann's heart, Jack arranges to rent a rather large truck with a canvas cover. He waits for the dirigible searchlights to depart from over the park, then he drives to where Ann directs him in the woods. Kong is nearly spent from his exertions. He has enough life left in him, though, to drag himself, following Ann, into the cover of the truck bed.

Jack drives while Ann treats Kong's wounds in the back of the truck with water and a first aid kit Jack had brought. They transport Kong off to –you might have guessed! –a recently constructed Primate Center in New Jersey that hasn't yet been opened to the public. The sympathetic director of the Center, Jane, takes immediately to Kong and offers sanctuary. Vets arrive to minister to his deeper wounds under signed oaths of secrecy.

To make an even longer (in my mind) better ending shorter: The Primate Center receives a large foundation grant and builds a Great Apes wing all for Kong, bringing in native flora and some of the least dangerous of native fauna from Kong's island to the primate center. Ann's acting career soars; she marries Jack and eventually they have two kids that grow up to be ecologically sensitive and primate-friendly; their son Sam becomes a climatologist, and their daughter Dianne eventually becomes Jane's apprentice. Ann visits Kong every weekend at the Primate Center.

Jane teaches Kong ASL sign language, for which he displays an amazing aptitude due to his evolutionary adaptation as a Giant Pongid along with his determination to be able to communicate with Ann!

Kong contributes to greater human understanding by communicating about his own insights and feelings, allowing humans to develop a greater understanding of the natural world Kong grew up in and to discover the loving, spiritual capacity of all of our primate cousins.

MY REFLECTIONS

In retrospect, I recognize that being an anthropologist I am particularly sensitive to the issue of saving endangered animals, especially our non-human primate cousins. I screamed, "No!" before stomping out of a theater many years ago when poachers were depicted about to butcher a gorilla in *Gorillas in the Mist*. That would surely be a good story to re-vision, in the world!

Movies like *Gorillas in the Mist* inform and make the audience aware of the sorts of atrocities humans are capable of in their lowest natures. But to truly change an outcome or influence cultural values, perhaps a widespread practice of the art of *Better Endings* could help! Although we might still feel powerless to alter the "big picture" on our own, if we practice better-endering in our own lives and help others to engage with creative re-visioning, then who knows? At least we might forge more mindful attitudes for ourselves and those we cherish.

Here also was a life lesson for me:

> *Do not go blindly into that Dark Fall. Don't kill off the wild nature that resides within yourself and others. How can I better celebrate and enhance Difference? How can I best embrace and foster my own wild side, my inner Kong?*

YOUR TURN

With the Better Endings Story Seed at the end of this chapter, I invite you to compose a list of 3-5 movies from films of any genre that have conclusions you have always either loved to hate or hated to love. After you have generated your list, please read over the titles, and circle the story for which you would most like to compose a *better ending*. Then in the lined journaling pages that follow and/or in your Better Endings Journal, you can envision and compose your own new conclusion for the story you have selected. The Story Seed prompts at the end of the chapter will guide you through your journaling process.

I encourage you to re-envision *better endings* for several stories on your list. You can also try your hand at imagining two or more alternative endings for the same story.

Remember, no one else needs to ever read your new version; this is for you. So, feel free exercise your full creative license!

For inspiration on how to arrive at *better ending* ideas, you can ask yourself: "What would happen IF...?" and "What then?"

Remember to include your personal thoughts about your *better endings* story ideas in the My Reflections sections provided, and/or in your Better Endings Journal. You can ask yourself: Why did I choose this (or these) stories? Why did I change it in the specific way that I did? What lessons can I take away from this *better ending* scenario for my own self-awareness and insight? Are there implications from my reimagined story ending for my own past, present or future actions and choices?

CLOSING THOUGHTS

Kong lives, for me, forevermore. With a more personally satisfying conclusion to the *King Kong* story, reviling or killing the Other no longer seems either necessary or ethical.

When you engage in creative re-visioning by re-scripting a bad (to you) movie ending, you illuminate an alternative, parallel world. Some quantum physicists now believe that every conceivable scenario might actually co-exist, in multiple or parallel universes. This book's Story Seed journaling prompts invite you to improve upon what you might perceive as messy or misshapen constructions of reality, at least to you; to wrest from them some 'better,' positive potentials.

Once you have altered your imaginative fabric of reality in this way, the new vistas you forge remain etched in your cognitive outlook. While I may never watch Peter Jackson's *King Kong* again, I can always revisit the Living Kong in my imagination or perhaps in my dreams. Indeed, now that you have read my 'Kong Lives!' story, your understanding of this tale's positive potentials has expanded.

Changing a story adds new tinctures to the fabric of reality, at least for the storyteller and their prospective readers, ever more. I encourage you to use the chapter ending Story Seed prompts in this book to freely engage with your own positive creative capacity, adding your personally re-visioned *better endings* to the stock in trade of story scenarios "out there."

Now then, as fiction authors might rightly protest, the *better endings* that you or I fabricate are not necessarily better fiction or better writing, nor are they intended to be. Good fiction writing portrays conflict and unfolds dramatic tensions that result in whatever sort of ending an author deems appropriate to the character arcs and plot development of their story; and clearly fiction authors apply their craft and exercise their artistic sensibilities with generally a greater virtuosity and artistry than others. Besides, their story is indeed their own and is, in that sense, inviolable.

We can revere good fiction writing while at the same time feeling free to alter a storyline for the purpose of self-exploration or to practice creative re-visioning for its own sake. Applying the principle of Better Endings grants you the flexibility to construe of reality as YOU might prefer it to be!

I encourage you with the Story Seed prompts below to envision and have fun composing one or more *better ending* movie conclusions before moving on to the next chapter.

Better Endings Story Seed

From Bitter to Better Endings: *At the Movies*

1. Make a list below of 3-5 popular films which you feel would benefit from *better endings*. Circle the title of the story you would most like to revise.

2. Write your story in the pages provided below, and/or in your Better Endings Journal.
3. Compose a New Story title (e.g., "Kong Lives!") that expresses your *better ending* movie story idea.

4. You may also use the pages provided below, and/or your Better Endings Journal to compose *better endings* for other films on your list, and/or create alternate endings for the same film.

My Reflections

After composing your *better endings* story or stories, write your personal reflections about what you have learned from engaging with this creative process.

Chapter 2

Movie Sequels Not Yet Made

Another way to apply the principle of Better Endings to popular movie endings is to imagine sequels to movies that seem to call out for them but which no one has yet produced. This is a blank canvas for your *better endings* practice, and if you happen to be a screenwriter or aim to become one, and you want to pitch your sequel idea, all the better!

For example, haven't you wondered what Mr. Roy Neary had in store when he stepped aboard the Mother Ship at the finale of *Close Encounters of the Third Kind*? What might your script for this movie sequel reveal about your own perspective on the story's potentials?

MY TURN

Here is my take on a sequel idea for *Close Encounters of the Third Kind*:

Mr. Neary Returns

Roy Neary eventually returns to Earth to conduct a mission of galactic proportions after his extraterrestrial companions have instructed and enlightened him over several earthly decades. Roy has not aged much while folks on Earth have, because the ship he has been traveling on regularly approaches light speed.

Mr. Neary was chosen carefully; he was the one of many called who arrived by his own free will and fortitude at the Devil's Tower spaceport to be whisked away for a higher level of education than he could ever have received on planet Earth. Roy was recruited telepathically to become an interplanetary ambassador at a time when Earthlings were just beginning to take baby steps toward joining the wider galactic community.

Roy's mission upon his return is to prepare Earthlings for their ventures into interstellar exploration and colonization. He delivers technological knowledge we can use to launch an exciting new age of galactic travel and interaction with other planetary lifeforms and civilizations. He also presents a galactic citizens constitution at a major U.N. convocation that heads of state and the peoples of all nations on Earth must agree to abide by in perpetuity; any non-peaceful actions in space will be immediately identified and thwarted.

MY REFLECTIONS

Think of all the fun potentials for a *Return of Mr. Neary* script! We can discover who that deerlike alien was who first greeted humans at the spaceport, along with who the cute little E.T. beings are who escorted Roy up the rampway into the Mother Ship. Why do they look so much like the little boy who was whisked away and then returned to his mom in the first movie?

I should ask myself (and please, do ask yourself after you have imagined a story-sequel plotline), why have I chosen this particular story to expand? I have always found science fiction compelling. I like the element of freedom offered in science fiction; the freedom for the story and its characters to realize possibilities not available in the world or society around me. Science fiction—when not dystopian—can and often does offer the sorts of *better endings* scenarios that its authors wish to see in the world. Utopian visions are often conveyed through the vehicle of science fiction. In fact, much of our current, 'real' science and technology have been directly influenced by prophetic or futuristic visions from science fiction such as from Star Trek or the futuristic works of H.G. Wells, Ray Bradbury, or Isaac Asimov.

Still, what is it about Roy Neary's space excursion with aliens and his prospective earthly mission that leads me in particular to contemplate his further adventures? I identify with Roy Neary's sense of being called to pursue a pathway to truth that is generally denied or hidden from public knowledge in our primarily materialistic society. I would relish being whisked away to discover what lies beyond the shadowy cocoon of earthly existence. I would also love to serve humanity by helping to usher in an era of higher consciousness. Hence my interest in developing the journaling tools with this book, to potentially foster *better endings* for all!

YOUR TURN

In the Better Endings Story Seed section at the end of this chapter, make a list of three to five movies that call out to you for a sequel. Circle a title, the sequel for which you would most like to see. Create a new title for what the sequel could be. For example, for *Close Encounters of the Third Kind*, my sequel title is *"Mr. Neary Returns."*

Next, imagine a natural seeming plotline for the movie sequel that you would like to see. What happens in the sequel story as you imagine for it to unfold?

Write out your sequel story idea.

You could also try your hand at some of the other movie sequel prospects you have listed, or you can devise two or more alternative sequel plots for the same movie to explore variable potentials of a single story.

YOUR REFLECTIONS

After you have composed your Better Endings movie sequel story or you have written alternate movie sequel storylines, be sure to add your *My Reflections* thoughts about what you have learned from this process of applying a better endings perspective to the story.

Why did you choose this specific movie for which to imagine a sequel? What might the original story, and your envisioned sequel plot, reveal about your own life experiences and interests or perhaps about your hopes and fears about your own or more general future potentials?

The exercise of imagining unmade sequels for a movie is like going to a film where you get to select which of several endings you wish to see. Can you apply this idea to where you stand in your life now, or with respect to some situation from your past, or in your possible future? What might have occurred other than how things did transpire? What different directions might current circumstances lead to for you and others concerned?

What would your best path forward be for some significant situation or concern? What actions can you take, now or in the near foreseeable future, to set your most desirable 'sequel' scenario into motion?

Use your *My Reflections* journaling section freely explore and flesh out your own future desires and insights.

CLOSING THOUGHTS

How might creatively envisioning a popular movie sequel apply to advancing your own optimal life story? How might your own further adventures unfold in relation to current situations and relationships? Do you like the direction things are going or would you like to tweak them a bit? How might you imagine *better ending* sequels for your unfolding—past, current or to come—situations?

For example, a personal story sequel I can envision would involve returning to visit with some close friends from earlier life phases, to share with them about what has happened with each of us since we knew each other before.

As a senior in high school, I designed a screenplay called "Through the Years," about a set of four high school friends who agree to meet at a specific place ten years later to share about what has happened to them over the next decade of their lives. In Act One as the friends are at their graduation ceremony from high school they talk about their future goals and set a date for their ten-year reunion. Act Two explores what actually transpires with each of the four pairs of these friends with some of their later partners, through the years. We discover in Act Two who successfully attains their high school goals, who changes their ambitions by making positive, flexible choices, and which of them falls short of attaining their life aspirations. Act Three brings the friends back together for their ten-year reunion, where they share with each other how their lives have progressed, or not so much for some of them, through the years.

In my script, the sequel story told in Act Three reveals that those with the most altruistic or deeply fulfilling goals and with the truest relationships are the ones who have attained their greatest happiness, whether they have actualized their high-school aspirations or developed new goals and other careers, through the years.

I encourage you to playfully imagine one or more *better ending* movie sequel stories based on the Better Endings Story Seed prompts below. Be sure to add your personal reflections before moving on to the next chapter.

Better Endings Story Seed

Movie Sequels Not Yet Made

1. Make a list of 3-5 popular films which you feel would benefit from movie sequels. Circle the title of the sequel story or stories you would most like to see.

_____

_____

_____

_____

_____

2. Write out your story sequel idea(s).
3. Create a Movie Sequel title for your new story idea(s).

_____

_____

_____

_____

_____

My Reflections

Journal about why you selected this story or this set of stories to add sequels for; what might these story sequels reveal about your own ambitions and interests? What do your sequel ideas for these movies reveal about your own life potentials and goals?

Chapter 3

Literary Transformations

I wrote my Masters thesis in linguistics about James Joyce's "Eveline," the opening story his *Dubliners* book of short stories. Eveline is a young Irish woman in 1914 Ireland. Her mother has died several years prior to the action of the story. It has fallen on Eveline to take care of her father and brothers ever since. But now a sailor from another country, Frank, has romanced Eveline and he offers to take her away with him, to Buenos Aires.

> *"She sat at the window watching the evening invade the avenue. Her head was leaned against the window curtains and in her nostrils was the odour of dusty cretonne. She was tired."*

So opens James Joyce's story of "Eveline." The question Joyce poses with his ten-page short story is simple: Will Eveline be able to leave family, Church and nation to go away with a foreigner to live in another land? Buenos Aires, meaning "good" or fresh "air," contrasts with the "dusty" but familiar air of Eveline's father's home in Dublin. There is hardly really a question of whether Eveline will leave; to Joyce, she cannot. By the end, when the moment for her to act arrives with the boat on which Frank has bought them passage, Joyce's Eveline is cast in a state of near paralysis:

> *"He rushed beyond the barrier and called to her to follow. He was shouted at to go on but he still called to her. She set her white face to him, passive, like a helpless animal. Her eyes gave him no sign of love or farewell or recognition."*

My re-visioned, *better endings* version of a conclusion for "Eveline" transpires in contemporary Ireland, where 62% of the population are urbanized and globalization offers many options to the youth for overseas emigration and jobs.

"Eveline" Revisited

Eve stands at the railing of the *Odyssey's* prow, straining to find Frank's face in the harbor crowd as the boat's powerful engines pull her away from the shore. Why has he not come? She reaches into the deep pocket of her windbreaker, palming the passage stub, a misty rain in the morning air obscuring her view of all she is leaving: her father, the rocky countryside, the steeple of the church she has attended since baptism. She grasps her woven purse, secure in her pocket with the money she has saved from weekly allowances over the last thirteen years.

Eve covers her forehead with the windbreaker hood and ties it so only her eyes are exposed. She is shaking; is it from the chill air? She turns away from the rail and climbs down the wooden steps from the prow into the passenger deck.

Ten or twelve huddled tourists peer out from their narrow windows, happy to be safe and dry. Eve, drenched from her watch above, gazes out the open window from her pew seat.

East is her direction now. Her new life opens before her.

MY REFLECTIONS

Modern or, more accurately, postmodern literary theory is about "deconstructing" literary texts. Why does an author use a certain tone of voice or how do they represent a certain bias, for example, based on their personal milieu and cultural background factors? James Joyce portrays his Eveline as "passive, like a helpless animal" to represent the stultifying influence of family, gender inequalities, nation and Church in early 20th Century Ireland.

Composing literary *better endings* lets me "re-construct" a text, to reshape a literary character or plot more in keeping with how or where my own imagination chooses to take the story.

My Eve breaks free from traditional Irish gender standards. The image of Eve rain-drenched on the prow of a ship departing from her familiar homeland is based on the real experience I had on a rainy day on the prow of a boat passing beneath the cliffs of Moher while visiting Ireland several years ago. Did my trip to Ireland lead to a liberating experience in my own life? Yes! It was just a few months after returning from that that trip that I began actively planning to retire early and relocate, far away from my home in Colorado after twenty-five years, which I did accomplish then in only two more years.

I never realized how transformative my trip to Ireland had been until journaling my reflections here about my *better ending* story of Eve!

YOUR TURN

The Better Ending Story Seed at the end of this chapter invites you to think of one or more fictional stories that have endings you wish you could rewrite more to your own liking. Maybe there is a whole genre of literature for which you'd love to insert a new formula; for example, maybe you would like the perpetrator in a who-done-it novel to find their come-uppance in some unusual manner that leads to an unexpected twist of outcome you would enjoy for this genre. Or maybe the "ever-after" story of a fairy tale couple is not quite so blithely happy ever after? This is the premise of Stephen Sondheim's musical *Into the Woods*: what really unwinds for each of the fairytale characters in Act IV, revealing the true basis of happiness?

So, make your list! What are 3-5 works of fiction (whether novels, poetry, short stories or plays) the endings of which you would just love to creatively toy with? Use the Story Seed prompts for this chapter below to develop your literary transformation ideas. Then go ahead; transform that story ending.

Make It Yours!

YOUR REFLECTIONS

After you have written your literary transformation *better endings* story, be sure to take time to further reflect on why you chose to transform this specific story. What is it about the original narrative that led you to want to make a change? How do your current—or earlier? —life conditions compare with the plot line or character arc of the original story?

How might changing this story inspire you to change or tweak some element of your own character or storyline? What about your life story could use some tweaking so you might ultimately arrive at living more fully the life you would imagine for yourself? What steps can you take now, or in the near foreseeable future, to bring about the sorts of new conditions you have envisioned for the character of the story you have changed?

CLOSING THOUGHTS

Transforming a literary ending to a story can lead to a transformative new direction in your own life. "Change a story, change a life: yours!" can be facilitated by identifying some element of what you are not entirely satisfied with in your own life playing out in a fictional world, then 'changing it up.'

Sometimes it is easier to imagine a creative twist to a work of fiction than it may be to recognize how you are yearning for a twist of fate in your own life circumstances. If you can imagine a more satisfying ending for a fictional story, then you have the capacity to shift your own life in a new direction. *Better endings* lead to new beginnings!

Better Endings Story Seed

Literary Transformations

1. Make a list of 3-5 fictional stories that you feel would benefit from *better endings*. Circle the story you would most like to transform.

_____

_____

_____

_____

_____

2. Compose your literary transformation story in your Better Endings Journal.
3. Create a title for your *better ending* literary transformation story.

_____

_____

_____

_____

_____

My Reflections

Journal about why you might have chosen these specific stories to transform. Do their original endings reflect something about how your own life story has been progressing? What actions can you take now or in the near foreseeable future to steer your own tale more in the direction of your narrative transformation story's *better ending*?

_____

_____

_____

_____

_____

_____

_____

_____

_____

_____

_____

_____

_____

_____

Chapter 4

What Then? Narrative Postludes

Depending on the point at which an actual or sometimes a fictionalized "true story" reaches its narrative conclusion, sometimes the viewer or reader is informed about what becomes of the main protagonists of the story in their futures. We learn who survives and not, and who goes forward in their life to apply what they have gained from their experience, or not. Certain genres of narrative including historically based stories are most subject to the inclusion of postludes. War movies often chronicle in their postludes what has become of the survivors of heroic events. Natural disaster stories might likewise reveal the future biographies of the survivors.

I invite you with this chapter to imagine postludes for one or more popular stories that have not originally included these. Then you can take your turn at applying the postlude device to your own and perhaps some of your family or significant others' future life potentials. It can be especially enlightening to play with what your personal postlude tale might look like first from the perspective of your current life trajectory and then, rather, if you were take some slight turn in a new direction.

MY TURN

Below are my examples of imagined postludes for two stories I feel could benefit from them.

Castaway

Chuck Noland married Bettina Peterson, the artist whose angel wings logo on a FedEx package had helped Chuck to survive and ultimately to escape from his five-year ordeal on a tropical island. Chuck later published his best-selling memoir, *"I'll Be Back!"*

Kelly Frear (Chuck's fiancé at the time of his plane crash) divorced her husband after their first daughter left for college. She returned to graduate school in psychology, where she earned her Ph.D. and became a successful family psychotherapist.

Contact

Dr. Eleanor (Ellie) Arroway married Father Paul Joss and they adopted two children from Puerto Rico. They co-authored *Ockham's Razor*—a book integrating their scientific and religious experiences—, which launched a popular movement dedicated to better preparing humanity for its next steps in extra-terrestrial communication and travel. When Ellie was 78, the alien race that had initially contacted her broadcast a friendly greeting to Earth on a global news station. Ellie was chosen to serve as Earth's ambassador, ushering in a brave new era of intra-galactic discovery and expansion of

Earth colonies through employing advanced interstellar transportation technology provided by the extraterrestrials.

How might you apply the tool of transformational postludes to your own life story narrative? Based first on where you are at in your current life, and then again based on what course your life might take by adding some element of change, what might your postlude reveal?

For example, if I were writing my postlude today, it would include the following:

Linda retired and relocated from Colorado to New York state, nearer to two of her sisters and her brother. Ultimately, she returned to her beloved high school hometown: a small, artistic village in western New York. She continued to teach online for several years. She published a series of journaling-based self-discovery books, along with a science fiction quatrain about the art of spiritual dreaming. Linda lived happily for many years with her dog Sophie and cat Emily in New York.

Now, here's the rub. To practice transformative postlude projections, remember it helps to first consider what your future life trajectory appears to be based on your current life conditions. Then, choose at least one thing that you could realistically "change up," now or in the near foreseeable future. Envision a change that would introduce a slight twist to your current life routines or that lets you begin to manifest some desired new activity or change of direction for your life. Revise your transformative postlude then, as if this new set of conditions has occurred.

I initially wrote the postlude I have shared above just before retiring. In that earlier postlude projection, I did not foresee relocating to my hometown. I added that idea into my postlude two years later, after I had already retired and relocated elsewhere. Realizing that my heart truly was wanting to be 'home,' I sold my house and moved yet again, within a year. This move has been an absolute delight and has positively transformed how I am moving forward with greater personal fulfillment.

My Reflections

It is well accepted in current popular psychology that the past is malleable. In psychotherapy or via other modes of memory re-scripting, we can modify our understanding or interpretation of even the most negative or traumatic past events so that their impact is less inhibiting to our future development. We can rescript our memories by revisiting significant events using active imagination, bringing our more mature, later perspective with us to review and even to alter the traumatic memory itself by re-visioning or journaling a meaningful dialogue with others involved in the memory.

We can likewise easily picture the future as in motion or "not written in stone." The future is an arc of unlimited possibilities conditioned in large part by our present attitudes and actions. Assuming that our future is not indelibly fated in advance allows us the flexibility to adapt and to conceive of more desirable future outcomes.

Why is it, though, that while we might consider the past and future to be somewhat malleable at least in our imagination, we experience the present as fixed and relatively immutable? We might feel 'stuck' or 'locked into' certain fixed routines that constrain and limit our actions and sap our motivations.

It is the present that most affects both our reflections on the past and our prospection or anticipation of the future. Therefore, the more we can focus on being flexible with our present conditions, the better we will be able to set into motion new pathways to pursue and fulfill our dreams!

YOUR TURN

Using the prompts in the Better Endings Story Seed section at the end of this chapter, compose your list of 3-5 popular stories that you feel would benefit from adding meaningful postludes. How might these stories unwind into the future based on where the key characters have arrived at in their lives by the end of the story as given? What are your wishes for or expectations about these characters? Which are likely to reach their greater happiness, and which appear destined for downfalls?

Compose a set of narrative postlude descriptions for one or more of the stories you have listed in the pages provided below, and/or in your Better Endings Journal (see the Story Seed below). You could also compose multiple, alternate same character postludes for the same story to explore different future potentials for the characters.

YOUR REFLECTIONS

Journal in the pages provided below and/or in your Better Endings Journal about what envisioning one or more narrative postludes for popular stories has revealed to you about how life may unfold from a current set of circumstances into future conditions.

Include in your reflections about narrative postludes some thoughts about what your own postlude might be like in the future, based on your and your significant others' current life conditions and choices.

What might change or what could you do to tweak some element of your life now or in the near foreseeable future that could set into motion a very different postlude about your own life story from some future perspective looking back? Is that altered postlude more, or less, desirable from the one you are living into now?

How would your ideal postlude about you and your significant others read? What are you willing and able to do realistically to manifest the core values of that future projection?

CLOSING THOUGHTS

I have always found it interesting to read or view the postludes of historical books or films. Some of the characters and historical figures went on to fulfill their ambitions; some attained comfortable but quiet lives; some died of terminal illnesses instead of achieving their life ambitions. The stories preceding these postludes, which were the bodies of the stories told, retrospectively provided the meaningful context for later life developments.

Envisioning transformative postlude scenarios about your own life trajectory allows you to imagine how a significant alteration to your present life conditions could lead to radical change over time.

Living our lives mindfully, with an awareness of how past-present-future forms a seamless web of interdependent events and their consequences, rather than living in a tiny bubble of the immediate present, can help us to bring about the sorts of *better ending* postludes that would make sense of a life well lived.

Better Endings Story Seed

Narrative Postludes

1. Make a list of 3-5 popular stories that you feel would benefit from meaningful narrative postludes.

_____

_____

_____

_____

_____

2. Write a set of character postludes for your selected story, or for multiple stories, or you could script alternate possible postludes for the same story in the pages provided below and/ or in your Better Endings Journal.

My Reflections

Journal about what the postludes you have envisioned reveal about how events or circumstances can set up future life conditions. What would your postlude story about your own life be like from the point of view of your present circumstances? How might your life story postlude change if you were to modify some element of your present life choices?

_____

_____

_____

_____

_____

_____

_____

_____

_____

_____

_____

_____

_____

_____

_____

Chapter 5

Endings You Already Love

W hat about those stories that you love in part for their already satisfying endings? Have you ever wondered why? Do these stories ring true or make sense in relation to your own life values and goals? Let's explore this dimension of story endings that you already love.

You can explore the sorts of story endings you love by creating a list of movies and fictional stories you enjoy, then writing brief synopses of their endings in the pages provided below, and/or in your Better Endings Journal (see the Better Endings Story Seed at the end of this chapter for journaling prompts.)

MY TURN

Here are brief synopses of three of my all-time favorite story endings:

Lord of the Rings (by J.R.R. Tolkien): In the final scene of *The Return of the King*, Frodo joins Gandalf, Bilbo Baggins and several elves on an ocean vessel heading off across the known horizons to the Undying Lands, far from the hobbit Shire. This scene always reminds me of the *I Ching* image of "crossing the Great Waters." The adventure never ends!

Lost Horizon (by James Hilton): Robert Conway returns to assume the abbot's role at Shangri-La, engaging on and finally completing a challenging, several months trek through the snowy Himalayan Mountain wilderness. Nearly spent from his arduous journey, Conway turns a corner and sees the beautiful Shangri La valley below and hears its enchanting music. His romantic interest, Sonya, is waiting for him there.

Harry Potter (by J. K. Rowling): Each of the key protagonist friends Harry, Hermione, and Ron have achieved deeply fulfilling transformations of character from engaging their trials and tribulations through their seven challenging years at Hogwarts School of Witchcraft and Wizardry that culminated with the Battle of Hogwarts. Harry fulfills his prophesized destiny as the 'chosen one,' defeating the evil Voldemort once and for all. Harry faces and overcomes his deepest fears, of death and of his own dark potentials, as he vanquishes the negative powers of Voldemort not only in the world but in himself. Harry tosses away the emblems of power he could have assumed with his victory, ultimately realizing the integrity of his deeper self. The final scene reveals Harry and the rest of the ensemble cast of friends twenty years later. Harry has become a loving parent (with his wife, Ginny Weasley) and he serves as head auror at the Ministry of Magic, sharing his wisdom with the next generations of wizards and muggles alike.

MY REFLECTIONS

All the stories on my list of favorite endings have fantasy or science fiction adventure components, as this is my favorite fictional genre. They all follow the three-stage plot structure of what Joseph Campbell has described as heroic adventures: departure, tribulations, and fulfillment or Return. These all are transformational stories, with their key protagonists undergoing challenging rites of passage to arrive at more mature and better integrated selves.

Like Frodo and Robert Conway, I always want for my adventures to never really end but instead to morph into even grander departures into the Unknown. Like Harry, Hermione and Ron I value the continuity of loving friendships above any material rewards. Adding *Contact* into the mix of stories with endings I love, like Eleanor Arroway (what a terrific surname!), I know there is always yet another "small step" to take and that blending my spiritual experiences with empirical knowledge carries me forward with a sense of life affirming purpose and meaning.

YOUR TURN

What are some story endings you already love? Are there common elements these story endings share, or do they represent a repertoire of possibilities that feel harmonious with your own life experiences and desires?

Make your list from the Better Endings Story Seed prompts below! Compose your synopses of these stories with endings you already love in the pages provided below, and/or in your Better Endings Journal. Highlight those aspects of these satisfying endings that you find most illuminating about the story or most compelling to your own life ambitions

Your Reflections

Do these story endings that you already love bring their characters a sense of meaningful closure after the saga of challenging ordeals they have endured and overcome? Can you relate? How so?

Journal about how you have achieved meaningful closure regarding challenging situations or chapters from your own life story. Are there situations or relationships about which you are still seeking closure?

Reflect about the value of satisfying endings and about your own capacity to bring them about. Imagine or write a synopsis of a meaningful closure you seek in your own life. What actions could you take now or in the near foreseeable future to facilitate a *better ending* for some nagging situation in your current life circumstances?

Were one or more of your earlier life episodes somewhat less than neatly resolved? How might these past situations have arrived at *better endings*? Are there lessons from such retrospective re-visioning that you could apply to unresolved situations of today or in your foreseeable future?

Closing Thoughts

It is good to discover, in fiction as in life, that many stories and life situations do resolve in ways that bring meaning to suffering or fulfillment to one's striving to realize heartfelt dreams.

Closure sets into motion new energies and opens pathways for new adventures to unfold. Whether we think of our life paths as composed of stages or recurring cycles or even as seamless threads full of surprising opportunities and challenges, we aim to find our adventure meaningful with every turn in the road along the way.

As an anthropologist, I like to think of the human species as *Homo Narrativus*: we are storytellers; what else? We build our lives with bricks of meaning that we derive mainly from those turning point events that mark our passages from childhood through our adult lives. Each of our lives as well as each momentous occasion within our lives is shot through with meaning, with goals and purpose, and with lessons we grow by and might also share with others.

The meaningful, satisfying endings of stories we love to read or see on the screen or tell from our own lives are markers of growth, change and development. They model for us how we can wind our way forward, step by step along the journey that leads to our highest fulfillment.

Better Endings Story Seed

Story Endings You Already Love

1. Make a list of 3-5 fictional stories whose endings you already love.

   _____

   _____

   _____

   _____

   _____

2. Write synopses of one or more of these stories' endings in the pages provided below, and/or in your Better Endings Journal.

My Reflections

Journal freely about why you find these specific story endings to be particularly satisfying, for you. Are there commonalities in these endings that you find personally appealing in relation to your own goals and values? Are there situations you have resolved well, or that you have yet to bring closure to, in your life? Compose synopses of what satisfying endings might look like for these current and/or past situations.

Chapter 6

History? Schmistory!

No fictional storylines are exempt from your capacity to retell or to creatively re-vision as you please. How does this feel to you? Are you beginning to sense how your inborn creative license is real and of potentially great value? Well then, let's venture forth to yet another dimension of storytelling: the oft-deemed taboo realm of rewriting history.

As an early entry for a blog site I have been writing for nearly a decade called *Better Endings* (yes, the inspiration for this book, at betterendingsnow.com), I posted a re-visioning tale for the history of the Titanic:

What might have happened differently if the Titanic had escaped its terrible encounter with destiny? Whether in some parallel world or from a slight tweak of human actions, the Titanic could have evaded the tragedy as well as the global despair that shades our collective memory of that disaster with an iconic, archetypal meme. We speak of the potentially "titanic" failure of any hopeful maiden voyage:

of a relationship, for instance, or of any creative venture with high stakes involved. So, let's re-vision a meme.

News Flash, 'The Old Post' (April 12, 1912)

The maiden Titanic truly proved herself unsinkable on an otherwise fateful night. Early this morning on the North Atlantic Ocean at 2:20 AM, Captain Edward Smith, reportedly responding to an inner nudge inspired by an eerie dream, chose to alter the Titanic ship's course on this moonless night just in time to slide past an ominous appearing iceberg! Passengers may count their blessings; many are bound to America to emigrate or to enjoy the beauty and bounty of our precious shores.

And what might have been a noteworthy result of such a slight twist of fate? Perhaps there was a young immigrant, Jack Dawson, who would have drowned had the Titanic not averted the iceberg, in a noble attempt to save the life of the upper crust girlfriend he had romantically entwined on the voyage, Rose Bukater. Postlude: Survivor Jack arrived in New York and enrolled at Columbia University on an immigrant scholarship that Rose's family influence helped him to obtain. Jack Dawson later became a distinguished climatologist, the very man who several decades later, in 1948, alerted the world about the perils of global warming by presenting an historic speech at the newly formed United Nations. After this historic address, the UN forged a commission that set to work to effect changes in our commercial use of natural resources in every free nation of the world. Were it not for the energy pacts and accords instituted so effectively by the UN in those momentous times, today we might yet be reeling from wars and perilous health dangers resulting from our unmitigated reliance on fossil fuels!

MY REFLECTIONS

Assuming free will along with a *better endings* perspective of flexible, mindful awareness, many otherwise fateful seeming tragedies might potentially have been avoided. This leads me to revisit some of my own past choices of action that preceded downturns or less than optimal results in my own life history.

It is easy to claim, as many would, that I hold "no regrets" about anything from my past that has been, after all, long passed. I would not be who I am today if not for all the cumulative decisions and shifts of course along the way; and had I chosen any differently regarding major life decisions, I would not have arrived at many of the daily blessings I am truly so thankful for today. Yet, in retrospect if I am being honest with myself, I could have approached some of these key decisions differently, too, and still have achieved positive or even in some respects better outcomes.

The main lesson I take forward with my license to reimagine history is to approach significant current decisions or even momentary options more carefully in relation to all that has come before. For me, a keyword in that learning endeavor has been patience. I am learning to avoid making mistakes of brash behavior that sometimes in the past led me to walk away from situations that in retrospect could have been more fruitful, had I been patient enough to see a situation through or to directly confront misunderstandings.

The old adage about making lemonade of lemons might seem fine to proclaim after having settled for less than "what could have been." But going forward in a truer, kinder, or more productive or proactive way calls for the best I have to give, in the moment.

"Did I do the best I could (then)?" Or "What am I being called to do (now)?" are considerations that can help me maintain a more flexible and responsive awareness that could be of value not only to myself but for others.

YOUR TURN

What critical historical events would you place highest on your list of significant historical situations you would like to creatively re-write? Do these historical events share common themes? If they are disasters, for instance, did they result from the decisions of those who suffered, or did uncontrollable natural calamities or other peoples' decisions bring them about, such as with hurricanes or international wars?

The Better Endings Story Seed prompts at the end of this chapter invite you to select one or more of these historical mishaps for which to compose your own *better endings* story or stories. Remember to include your insights about the retrospective consequences of what could have happened differently if only the tweaks of decision or fortune you identify with your revisionist history would have actually occurred.

YOUR REFLECTIONS

Is not to decide, to decide? What can you take away from rewriting history that also applies to your own life history and potential?

Reflect on your personal history. What turning point sorts of decisions did you make or actions did you take in a situation that, in retrospect, did not work out as well as it could have?

How might you be able to steer in a slightly different direction now, when faced with choices like those decisions from your past that you regret? Are there certain kinds of situations that you would like to handle differently when they come around again?

What might you think, say, or do differently if you had a significant conversation or decision to redo today? Use the pages provided below and/or your Better Endings Journal to explore questions such as these that could help you be more mindful when some new moment of choice comes around.

Closing Thoughts

Quick, singular decisions such as whether to pay attention to a warning and steer your ship clear of an iceberg, or else to vainly expect your state-of-the-art vessel will pass it by without incident, can change the world. Likewise, choosing to not have one more drink before driving, or thinking twice about expressing an unwelcome remark, could also alter history for all concerned.

Responding from better judgement or from your most positive inner nudges can prevent titanic mishaps of fortune. Perhaps then, this playful exercise of rewriting history is not so frivolous or vain, after all, if it might help us to think twice or to step up with a positive, *better endings* action today.

Better Endings Story Seed

History Schmistory!

1. List 3-5 momentous situations from national or world history
   that you wish had either never occurred or had led to different
   results.

   _____

   _____

   _____

   _____

   _____

2. Circle one (or more) of the events you have listed and write
   a revisionist *better endings* story in the pages provided below,
   and/or in your Better Endings Journal. You could also
   compose multiple, alternate historical accounts for one of
   these events.

My Reflections

Journal your reflections about the revisionist history you have written. Is there anything about this reconstructed event that reminds you of situations in your own life history that you wish would have gone better, too? What lessons could you take away from this exercise in rethinking the past that can be of potential value to you, going forward?

Chapter 7

Heeding Omens

History is ripe with possibilities never fulfilled. What if we could presage and heed warnings about the course an event might take and act to prevent or preclude undesirable outcomes? Then we could proactively cultivate *better endings* before some potentially disastrous event would happen at all.

The idea of precluding events by heeding warning signs reminds me of Shakespeare's dramatic record of Julius Caesar's murder. "Beware the Ides of March!" said a soothsayer, warning Caesar outright of his portending doom. Then also Caesar's wife Pompeia awoke early on that fateful morning with a prophetic dream of her husband's imminent murder, beseeching Julius to avoid going to the senate that day. Had Caesar heeded those omens, he could have avoided his death on that day and possibly he could have taken actions to thwart the murderous plot based on his presaged knowledge.

The theme of heeding omens, or not, shows up in many popular stories.

I remember this was a regular feature in Dick Tracy cartoons that I watched on TV as a child. Dick's detective assistant, Joe Jitsu, would invariably get himself into big trouble so that, typically, some criminal's well aimed bullet would be headed directly at Joe's forehead. Joe would quickly touch and speak into his rather futuristic video wristband. All action—time itself—would immediately freeze while Joe conferred with Dick Tracy:

"Joe Jitsu, calling Dick Tracy. Come in, Dick!"

All action in the cartoon would remain frozen while Joe and Dick held a back-and-forth conversation about the dire situation Joe was facing. In the event of a bullet racing toward Joe, Dick would say something simple, like:

"Duck!"

Joe Jitsu would duck down then just before the action would flash back on, causing the bullet to whizz by harmlessly over his head. Then Joe would collar the unfortunate criminal.

So again, what if Julius Caesar had taken heed when both his soothsayer and his wife's dream had clearly predicted disaster on that fateful Ides of March? Likewise, with such episodes of history that tragically repeat, what if both Abe Lincoln and J.F.K. had heeded warnings? They both, too, are known to have received prescient omens that they chose not to heed. Had they recognized the truth in these omens, the "alti-verse" rest of the story then, with twists of possible consequence such as we imagined with the previous chapter on rewriting history, would be history instead!

MY TURN

For this theme of heeding dire warnings, I think immediately of an event from my own childhood; for, if this moment had not unfolded as it did, I would not be here!

Saved by Mom's Intuition

When I was four years old living with my family in Cincinnati, Ohio, my sister and brother and I were swimming in our backyard pool one quiet summer afternoon, when suddenly my mother yelled out to us from across the back yard:

"All of you, get out of the pool; come into the porch with me, now!"

Mom was seated in our screened porch, reading a book while monitoring us in the pool. She had noticed how, very quickly, dark storm clouds were amassing overhead; then in a flash of sudden awareness, she knew what was about to occur. We three kids immediately climbed out of the pool when she called us, and we ran into the screen porch with our mother, not knowing why she had called us out of the pool.

Within seconds of reaching the porch, a lightning bolt struck the pool's water!

MY REFLECTIONS

Certainly I have never forgotten nor have my brother and sister how our mother, Elizabeth Rugh Watts, heroically saved our lives that day. It could have so easily gone otherwise, but Mom paid attention to her flash of intuition and acted immediately. We survivors from childhood of this potentially tragic event are extremely fortunate beneficiaries of our mom's quick response to the omen of those fast-approaching storm clouds.

YOUR TURN

In the space provided with the Better Endings Story Seed section at the end of this chapter or in your Better Endings Journal, write your list of 3-5 historical, fictional, and/or autobiographical events that either did or would have turned out much for the better if some omen was recognized and heeded.

If you recall or know about events from your own or your family's life history when a potentially disastrous course of events was precluded by some alert action—like my Mom acting swiftly on her intuition—please include that on your list.

After circling one or more of the events on your list that you would like to focus on, compose your *better endings* tale or two in the pages provided below, and/or in your Better Endings Journal.

YOUR REFLECTIONS

What will you take away from this practice of reviewing or envisioning proactive twists of fate?

Have there been times when you have received a sign foretelling possible disaster or symbolically alerting you to a potentially wrong decision or action? What happened? Did you heed the warning and redirect your actions to avoid making a big mistake, or did you go ahead anyway? If you did not heed the signs, do you have reason to wish in retrospect that you had? What might you do to pay better attention, next time?

Write in the pages provided below and/or in your Better Endings Journal about how you tend to deal with your own inner nudges or outer warning signs. Is there some situation in your current life that you are questioning? How can you look for signs or answers to bring more clarity?

CLOSING THOUGHTS

Omens, warning signs, or inner nudges about a possibly wrong—or right—action could come in many different forms. When we are pondering an action or an important decision, we look for signs to help us navigate our course. Outer signs may include waking dreams. These occur as direct messages that come to us through casual remarks made even by a stranger, or that capture our attention on a billboard, on a TV commercial, or even on a license plate we are following behind.

Waking dream messages are forms of synchronicity, answering some question we have been mulling over with a very direct statement. "Be careful!" says a mother to her child at a grocery store reaching for some desired product on a shelf too high for her to reach; just as you have been asking yourself whether some action you are considering could overreach your means. The fact that you take notice and that you are exactly where you need to be in the moment to recognize such a message shows it is worth your paying attention.

Inner nudges, like my mother's intuitive flash of alarm, can guide us in the moment, too, so long as we are accepting enough to respond!

Following waking dream signs or responding to omens opens pathways to *better endings* that can steer our own lives forward, just as they do in fiction or on the big screen. The rest of this book's chapter topics, with Part Two starting next, will help you cast *better endings* light upon significant elements of your own life story.

I hope that by now you have engaged with the Better Endings Story Seeds at the ends of these chapters enough to realize your journaling and your personal reflections with this book can be personal Sandbox for creative re-visioning.

Better Endings Story Seed

Heeding Omens

1. List 3-5 stories that involve omens or signs, either from history or fiction, or from your own life history. These stories might involve an omen that was not heeded, or signs that were paid attention to with positive results.

_____

_____

_____

_____

_____

2. Circle one (or more) of the stories from your list and compose a *better endings* account. If the story already represents a *better ending* because the signs were heeded, describe how that happened and the results. You could also compose multiple, alternate accounts of the same story to explore a range of possible outcomes.

My Reflections

Write your reflections about heeding omens in the pages provided below, and/or in your Better Endings Journal. Have you had experiences where you did not—or, did—heed signs or omens? What happened? How might you recognize signs in the future?

PART TWO

Better Endings for
Your Life Story

Interlude

N ow for the rest of the *better endings* story…yours! Part Two journaling tools invite you to apply your inherent faculty of Better Endings to significant aspects of your own life story: past, present, and future.

Life is in its most dynamic form a transformational process of growth and development. We can never be too old or too young to reflect on our current circumstances or conditions and to contemplate and manifest transformative change along the way. Creative re-visioning and journaling about *better endings* engages your capacity to be flexible.

Again with the chapter topics in Part Two, I share brief examples to illuminate the theme and then the topic is yours to explore in the pages provided, and/or in your Better Endings Journal, to arrive at your personal insights. I share story examples from my own or others' commonplace life experiences not because these stories should matter to you but because every life matters; each of our life stories matter uniquely in the grand scheme of life. What you do in your life benefits your family and loved ones and expresses your distinctive flair to living.

I often say to my pets and to students, family members, and friends, that there has never been nor will there ever be again another you. Even our DNA structures are entirely unique, like fingerprints.

Margaret Mead famously remarked: "Always remember that you are absolutely unique. Just like everyone else."

What you bring to your world, no one else can bring. Therefore, the self-awareness you gain from your most meaningful growth and development benefits those around you by bringing inspiration and wisdom from which they too might grow. Socrates' sage admonition to "Know Thyself!" is truly wise. When we proceed mindfully in our everyday lives, learning as we go and being open to change and new opportunities, our world itself seems ever more expansive!

First then, as the opening topic for Part Two about applying the principle of Better Endings to your own life story, please consider how your life has been punctuated with shaping events, those pivotal moments or situations in your life that have influenced you to become the person you are today. Some of these shaping events were of such magnitude that you might feel you were a different person before and after that event occurred.

Let's begin your creative re-visioning of *better endings* in relation to your own life story by exploring the topic of Turning Points.

Better Endings Story Seed

Part Two Interlude: Better Endings for Your Life Story

As you prepare to explore experiences from your own life to benefit from your imaginative faculty for creative re-visioning, please take some time to reflect the writing space below or in your Better Endings Journal about your unique life story. What makes you, YOU?

Chapter 8

Turning Points

Turning Points set into motion key transitions in our lives. What might have happened differently if you had chosen to not join the armed forces (if you did), or if you had accepted that different kind of job offer that you declined? We might muse about such imponderable twists of fate or fortune. And well we should consider such turning point sorts of choices or happenstance, as none of us would be who we are today but for these significant turns in the road that opened—or closed—new pathways before us!

One way to apply the creative principle of Better Endings to turning points is to consider some recent or expected future decision in relation to how you have approached significant choices in the past. Any decision can lead to a *better endings* sort of turning point if it leads you to significantly "change things up" in a growth-enhancing, positive direction.

MY TURN: A Road Not Taken

Shortly before I was to complete my Ph.D. as a graduate student, a job position was created at a community college where I was teaching that was explicitly designed to suit my strengths, as the chair of the department had established this new faculty line to potentially hire me fulltime after I had been teaching there part-time for several years.

As with any faculty opening, the chair advertised it generally to allow qualified applicants to apply. The job description was narrowly framed, though, to limit the likely pool of applicants. I applied. Several people I knew who might also have applied held back because the job description was very specific for the sub-field of cultural anthropology. While the search was in progress an also all-but-doctorate archaeologist who had recently returned from working in Russia applied. Technically her archaeology specialization did not match the qualifications stated in the job description, but her work was politically prestigious. When the chair of the department learned of her application, she and I were ranked as equally "excellent" after very light interviews with basic questions. The president of the college then selected the archaeologist for the job, over my more appropriate levels of training and experience.

At first, I was upset and felt blindsided by this inappropriate hire. I raised the issue of the mismatched job qualifications at the administrative level. An official agreed I posed a valid complaint, so the Human Resources director offered me a choice. I could press my complaint one step further and it was likely the outcome of the search would be reversed; I would be hired. I contemplated my choice for days, considering all sides of the situation. What would my future look like if I would take this bold step, or not?

I chose to not press the complaint any further. I did meet with the department chair and protested the selection process as a violation of best practice procedures.

But that was all I did. I never taught again for that college after the current semester ended. In a few months I graduated with my Ph.D.

and quickly accepted a tenure-track professorship in Colorado, where I have taught since for over twenty-seven years.

My Reflections

Had I pressed the matter further at the community college, I might have had a less interesting and a less productive academic career at a community college rather than at my research and teaching based university post. I look back with gratitude at the choice I made then. Remembering this pivotal choice during later emotionally charged decision points has helped me turn down other potentially wrong choices as well.

Your Turn

Can you relate? Have you ever been denied a goal only to realize later it would not have been worth it for you to obtain? Or have you successfully pressed against the grain of some disappointment only to later wish you had not attained a reprieve in the situation, after all?

For the Better Endings Story Seed at the end of this chapter, make a list of three to five Turning Point decisions from your life, including at least one potential decision you face now or that you expect to face in the near foreseeable future. Write or talk about or actively contemplate the value of such shaping events in your life. For each, consider: how did this past event or how might this current situation become a *better endings* Turning Point for you? Journal in the pages provided below and/or in your Better Endings Journal about one or more of your earlier shaping events. Then for a current or anticipated future situation, consider where you are at now in relation to these earlier Turning Point moments, and compose a *better endings* scenario so that you may choose your path forward with wisdom.

YOUR REFLECTIONS

After you have composed *better endings* stories about one or more of your Turning Point choices reflect in the pages provided below, and/or in your Better Endings Journal about the lessons you take away from re-visioning your Turning Points. Does it seem that some of the critical Turning Points in your life were mainly brought about by others? Or did you make active choices too? When faced with similar situations going forward, is there anything you might choose to do differently to bring about *better endings* for all concerned?

CLOSING THOUGHTS

Decision points offer fertile grounds for seeding *better endings*. They bear gifts of opportunity to change things up! Along the road of life are many twists and turns, each posing opportunities to either go with the flow, without thought of your most beneficial outcomes, or to craft your future mindfully, proactively preparing for what is around the bend with care.

Our capacity for creative re-visioning to bring about *better endings* reveals to us our innate creative license, not just for playful reimagining of fiction or historical fact but for scripting our own life stories going forward. Remember this: No story matters more in the end than yours!

Better Endings Story Seed

Turning Points

1. Make a list of 3-5 shaping events or Turning Points from your life, including at least one event from your past and current situation you will be making a key decision about now or in the near foreseeable future.

_____

_____

_____

_____

_____

2. Circle one or more of the Turning Points in your list and write about them in the pages provided below, and/or in your Better Endings Journal. Explore the dynamics of these Turning Point events. You could also compose multiple, alternate accounts of either a past or future Turning Point to explore a range of possible outcomes.

My Reflections

Journal about how the Turning Points you have identified have shaped your life story. What decisions have positively affected your life? What decisions or situations might you have approached differently; what could have happened then? How can you approach future significant choices with greater foresight and wisdom?

Chapter 9

Big Moves

One common sort of Turning Point involves a Big Move, relocating either with your family or on your own for work or retirement or for continuing a relationship or simply for the adventure of experiencing another place to live. Big Moves offer great opportunities, yet they may also involve enormous challenges.

We could apply the principle of Better Endings to Big Moves in relation to before, during, or after the relocation occurs.

There could be significant "loose ends" to resolve before you would feel entirely free and ready to leave your current home or situation. How could you best prepare those you care about, and yourself, for your departure well enough in advance to allow for a smooth transition? In this era of easy connectivity through social media networks and communications devices that include face-to-face video calls, you may feel less of a need to sever your well-established ties these days than ever before.

During your Big Move, you will have opportunities throughout to be mindful with the choices before you every step of the way. Have you found the best location to establish your most desirable new life conditions? Have you managed your funding so you will be as comfortable as possible in your new work and living environment?

Have you left plenty of room for you and your loved ones' personal growth and for positive, transformative changes of lifestyle? You can network in advance of your move to set up some connections you would like to build upon as you reestablish yourself in your new environs.

After your Big Move you will find many tremendous, yet daunting, new opportunities opening before you. Transplanted in rich new soil, this is a time ripe for making well considered changes in your lifestyle, from small to large. Your entire presentation of self can be modified to the degree that you might choose to do so. Many people use Big Moves to carve out exciting new directions or pathways as they move forward with their lives. You can keep the best of what you have gained while you explore and forge fresh inroads to actualize your fullest potentials.

MY TURN: The Protean Self

Big Moves are very familiar to me. I grew up in a family which relocated often because my father was often transferred from one state to another or took jobs with different companies throughout his career as an aeronautics engineer. By the time I was 13 my family had relocated five times, from two cities in Ohio, to California when I was four, back to Ohio when I was five and then when I was seven we moved again, to Pennsylvania.

Approaching a move to a new state was difficult for me and my three sisters and brother. Losing touch with close friends and having to make new friends and step into a new school and unfamiliar home environment was never easy.

When Dad announced yet another Big Move to New York state when I was 13 in seventh grade, I realized then how moving offered me a tremendous opportunity to transform patterns I had fallen into as an awkward young teen in Pennsylvania. I was developing into somewhat of what would later be called a nerd in seventh grade, not at all one of the "popular" girls at my junior high school.

For an entire year as my parents prepared the family for our Big Move to New York, I consciously planned this time for a *better ending* metamorphosis. During that year in advance of the move I selected new, more fashionable clothing; I changed the way I wore my hair; and I told myself I would actively befriend more "popular" types at my new school.

After the move I initially sat at a lunch table with a set of girls I perceived to be in a "popular" clique. I even wore a ring (during lunch hour) borrowed from my mother's jewelry box to pretend with these girls that I had an older, out of state boyfriend!

The clique mildly accepted me, yet in short time I came to recognize how we had little in common in terms of mutual interests. I started avoiding even going to lunch then, hiding out in a stall in the girls' lavatory for the entire lunch period!

Gradually, I developed new, more appropriate friends. The people I naturally gravitated toward were artistic, creative and, yes, in retrospect we were all rather nerdy. As water finds its level, I came to relish my very active high school years in New York with a small set of dear, close friends.

MY REFLECTIONS

Ever since my family's Big Move from Pennsylvania to New York I have approached relocation as a golden opportunity for significant change and lifestyle choices to better suit my evolving interests, values, and goals. I learned from that early experience how to enact conscious choices to bring about positive change. I also learned how not every change I might think I am seeking from a move would be worthwhile in the long run. Quite likely, this was where the very notion of "better endings" first took root in me.

More recently, I retired except for online teaching and relocated from Colorado back to New York state, where over the next three years I have moved twice again to live in three different New York locations. I have used creative visualization, journaling, and online search tools to fully envision each next shift in location and lifestyle. The result was a gradual unfoldment of understanding that led me through two moves until finally I realized the great value to me of returning to my original hometown. In retrospect it was important for me to remain open and flexible throughout this transitional passage. Retiring and relocating have engaged me in a gradual progression of unfolding interests, leading me 'home' in a way I could not have predicted when the journey began.

YOUR TURN

What about the Big Moves in your life, including those already transpired and possibly yet to come? How do you tend to approach Big Moves; what does relocation mean, to you? Have you regarded moving primarily as interrupting or disrupting your established activities and friendships, or have you welcomed relocating for the opportunities to implement positive changes in your new way of life and environs?

In the space provided with the Better Endings Story Seed for this chapter below, make your list of three to five Big Moves from your life, including at least one that you are expecting to undertake at some point in your near or foreseeable future. Journal about at least one of your past moves and about your anticipated or wishful future relocation. Remember to apply the Better Endings principle especially to your prospective future

Big Move. Even if you have no current plans that involve physically relocating, you can still use this opportunity to journal about a fantasy move. This frees you to explore your hankering for changes, large or small, even if you would opt to find ways to introduce these tweaks into your current residence and location by moving 'in place.'

YOUR REFLECTIONS

After you have journaled about your Big Moves and future relocation or life-tweaking prospects in the pages provided below, and/or in your Better Endings Journal, be sure to add your personal reflections on the topic. What have you learned about yourself from reviewing past Big Moves? If you were compelled to relocate because of circumstances outside your control, such as when your parents moved to a location you did not want to go, how did you handle that? While you cannot undo such moves, were there good things that came from them, too?

Or maybe, as is true for many, you have lived in the same house or locality for all your life, and you have no desire to move or expectation of ever relocating. What other sorts of Big Moves have you experienced, instead, that have allowed you to grow and remain flexible in your home grounds? In this case, journaling or writing a *better endings* story about a fantasy move or about a grand travel expedition might reveal to you some inner yearnings. How can you fulfill those yearnings?

CLOSING THOUGHTS

Remember: You are the author as well as the core heroic adventurer in your own dynamic life story. You have the creative license to script and rescript your story as you will. Even if it feels like merely a wild flight of fancy, well then, open your fantasy wings, and soar! Imagination can be your golden key to transporting yourself from some relatively bitter corner in which a part of you feels stuck or stagnant to a lifestyle and locale where you can fulfill your most ardent, yet also practical life dream, and thrive!

Better Endings Story Seed

Big Moves

1. Make a list of 3-5 Big Moves in your life, including at least one anticipated or fantasy future move.

   _____

   _____

   _____

   _____

   _____

2. Circle at least one of these past Big Moves (if any) and at least one future or fantasy Big Move, and compose *better endings* stories around these in the pages provided below, and/ or in your Better Endings Journal. You could also compose multiple, alternate accounts for any one of these to explore a range of possible scenarios.

My Reflections

Explore your reflections about the topic of Big Moves in the pages provided below or in your Better Endings Journal. Consider your thoughts about this topic from several angles, including what you have learned about your yearnings for change even if that means introducing tweaks to your current home environment and lifestyle.

Chapter 10

Silver Linings

I t is often difficult to accept a major change in our life, especially when that change comes about not by our own choice but is imposed externally, either by our parents when we are young or by other persons or due to a cataclysmic natural event beyond our control. Applying the principle of Better Endings to re-visioning such critical change events allows us to find the proverbial silver lining of even the darkest cloud.

If we are laid off from our job, for example, we could decide to use the time out of work to retool and come back to the workforce stronger. If we encounter a challenging health condition, we might recognize how coping with this condition brings us valuable life lessons, loving care, and resources; or it may teach us how to treat ourselves more kindly.

Silver linings is a metaphor we can use to describe such realizations. Every dark cloud or apparently unmovable obstacle in our lives has its silver lining, its positive potential outcomes for growth and new opportunity. Too often it is in hindsight that we come to appreciate silver linings; while undergoing such dark nights of the soul ordeals, the clouds may be stormy indeed.

For this chapter's Better Endings Story Seed journaling time, I shall invite you to practice recognizing silver linings from some of your past and/or current life challenges.

MY TURN

A PBS program about the brain once aired an episode about a professional music conductor and pianist who suffered a brain lesion that resulted in complete short-term memory loss. Every day he would write in his journal, "Today is the first day of the rest of my life!" He could not hold onto a conversation or a memory from moment to moment.

However, there were two silver linings to this musician's traumatic brain injury. His wife would visit him at the hospital every day. He would not remember her consciously and yet he absolutely recognized her as someone he knew and loved. Every day when she stepped into his room he would exclaim: "Claire," (using her name, though I am fabricating one here) "it is so good to see you! I have not seen you forever!"

When this concert pianist who had lost his short-term memory sat down at a piano, although he could no longer read music that he was unfamiliar with from the page, he could play entire symphonies beautifully, fully immersed in the music. When he would finish a piece, he would shudder as if in a convulsion, shifting back cognitively to the blank screen of his memory-impaired condition.

Silver linings indeed! How many of us can say we have nearly as much momentary joy and absorptive appreciation of our loved ones or of music as this man enjoyed, as if for the first time, every time?

MY REFLECTIONS

Two people who experience similar challenging ordeals might respond very differently depending on whether they can or cannot appreciate silver linings.

For example, one person might regard an experience such as an illness or car accident or losing their job as a major calamity that sends them into a long-term downward spiral. Yet, very similar events could find a different person realizing how fortunate they were in retrospect that the illness or car accident or job loss occurred, because of circumstances that had unfolded since. These latter folks might declare how they would never have improved their long-term health or obtained that next job of their dreams if their earlier challenge had never occurred. Their flexible, optimistic attitudes lead them to not only celebrate silver linings but to benefit from their most challenging ordeals!

Attitudes matter. I know the sooner I can locate the silver linings of some unwinding ordeal, the better I can steer through the situation to arrive at more positive outcomes. If hindsight is twenty-twenty, so much the better to have the clarity of foresight that comes with recognizing silver linings as we proceed.

YOUR TURN

What have been some silver linings associated with challenging circumstances or events from your life: past, present, or that you anticipate could be lurking around the bend? Using the space provided in the Better Endings Story Seed section at the end of this chapter, compose your list of 3-5 difficult ordeals about which you either already have, or have not yet, recognized silver linings.

Explore in the pages provided below and/or in your Better Endings Journal about one or more of these core personal challenges. For a past situation, whether you were able to recognize its positive aspects then or not, what were some silver linings you can appreciate in retrospect now? Looking at a current hardship, or looking ahead to an anticipated daunting challenge, contemplate and journal about how you already have or could benefit from the gifts of silver linings available to you because of these challenges.

YOUR REFLECTIONS

After re-visioning and journaling about how silver linings have been present through some of your most daunting life situations, reflect on what has been or could be the value overall of recognizing silver linings in your life?

How can your attitude of gratitude for silver linings help you better accept change and bring about *better endings* in terms of more positive life conditions and circumstances?

CLOSING THOUGHTS

Change is a constant, though not always welcome. Flexibility is the greatest asset we may draw upon as we navigate through change from moment to moment, day by day. Appreciating the silver linings of our more difficult ordeals helps us develop a resilient attitude, more accepting of hardship and change.

If we can manage to squeeze some lemonade out from even the bitterest of life's lemons, we may yet find meaning and purpose in the most challenging times.

Better Endings Story Seed

Silver Linings

1. Make a list of 3-5 challenging situations from your life: past, ongoing, or anticipated in your near or foreseeable future.

_____

_____

_____

_____

_____

2. Circle one or more of the situations you have listed and explore their silver linings in the pages provided below, and/or in your Better Endings Journal. Compose your *better endings* account based on how these experiences have, or could yet, benefit you going forward.

My Reflections

Journal about how life's silver linings have helped you steer through some of your most difficult times. If those hardships had not occurred, where would you be without the silver linings these ordeals also brought into your life? Can you recognize silver linings of some anticipated future challenge in advance, to better prepare for the difficulties ahead?

Chapter 11

What If?

The standard question people use to activate a better endings mindset is the age-old question, "What If?" What if your father had slept in and skipped his usual morning walk in the park, so he had never met your mom? Then you, as the uniquely endowed genetic individual you are, would not be here at all!

On the other hand, what if sleeping in had caused your father to take a later than usual walk, which is how he met your mother, after all? Or what if your mother, on a sudden whim of intuition, had impulsively decided to wait for a later bus on the way to the park, where she met your dad?

This question of *'What If?'* is tantalizing. It invokes deeper philosophical and spiritual questions about fate versus free will or self-destination. Are our lives more a product of one or the other of these diametrically opposed principles of predestined fate versus self-destination? Do you feel bound to fate so that your life conditions seem immutable, or are you free to create your own *better ending* pathways winding forward?

MY TURN: Changing College Majors, New Pathways Forged

I have often asked myself where I would be today had any number of events or relationships never occurred or had they taken different courses. Let me try one on as an example.

What if as an undergrad in college I had not changed my original major of post-secondary education, first to English literature, then to linguistics for my Masters degree, and later again to anthropology for my doctoral program?

First off, I would likely have become a high school English teacher, which was my goal when I started college because of some excellent role models of English teachers who had inspired me. I would most likely have stayed in western New York for a long teaching career in a high school there; so, I would never have moved Out West to Arizona or done anthropological fieldwork and met excellent friends in Zuni, New Mexico. Nor would I have taught anthropology for twenty-five years in Colorado before moving Back East to western New York. I would not have met any of my graduate school and post-college friends or romantic interests who have been among my closest relations, nor my beloved pets who have been my primary home-away-from-home family for well over forty years.

Where would I be today? How might life have been different; yet too, how much about this other life might yet nearly be the same? Maybe I still would have discovered the spiritual path I practice. Maybe although I would not have met specific persons and pets, I would have connected with similar sorts of friends and partners and equally dear pet companions. Maybe I would yet be married, even possibly with children who by now would have children of their own. How much might any of these differences have really mattered, from the point of view of *better endings*?

MY REFLECTIONS

This exercise helps reveal to me what has mattered most in my life as compared with what has been less necessary or core to who I am on the deepest level.

Perhaps it is the kinds of experiences we have that matter more so than the specific people, places, or types and lengths of relationships encountered along the way? Still, it is difficult for me to conceive of not having met and spent glorious time with the primary people, places, and relations I have loved and enjoyed in life to now.

More specifically from the vantage point of *better endings*, how necessary or 'fated' might my decisions have been within those relationships and events that led to major Turning Point lessons, key insights of a lifetime? Maybe what matters is learning those life lessons well, so that the most challenging conditions do not have to keep repeating. I think that once I have learned a relationship lesson well, for instance, I have been able to then move on to better experiences.

I have always aimed to listen to my inner guidance along the way, so that my choices have generally not felt random or chaotic. Nevertheless, I certainly could have forged different pathways along the way; there are always alternative directions from which to choose. Have *better endings* consistently been a guiding consideration or have convenience or even fear sometimes interfered with my best possible choices?

To be honest with myself, I realize sometimes I have acted impulsively or based on weaknesses instead of stepping forward in the moment. In flight or fight moments, I have more typically opted for flight or withdrawal. This is one of my lessons. In retrospect I have made missteps along the way; most of them minor but some of them potentially huge.

I go ahead then, aiming to learn from my mistakes and not repeat them. Still, I am left with some imponderable *What Ifs?*

YOUR TURN

Before you proceed to the Better Endings Story Seed for this topic of *What Ifs*, allow me to introduce some common sorts of *"What If?"* scenarios. You could use one or more in your Story Seed responses if you like, or you can use your own instead. Try to arrive at a *better endings* outlook. How might things have gone better *if* some situation had unfolded differently; or, how might your life be better today had the *What If* you are re-visioning never occurred?

So, for example: *What If* one or both of your parents had made a critical decision that took themselves and your family in a major different direction while you were growing up? For example, if they had divorced, or if they had not divorced; or if they had taken you overseas as part of your childhood? How might your life story have turned out differently then? What could have been some *better endings* potentials from such twists of fate or fortune?

Or, as another example: *What If* you had chosen differently with respect to one or more of your major life choices involving careers, relationships, or places you have chosen to live? Remember to approach your musings about these *What If?* scenarios from a *better endings* perspective.

Now then, have at! Using the Better Endings Story Seed prompts below for this chapter, you can explore this topic of *What Ifs* in the pages provided below, and/or in your Better Endings Journal.

YOUR REFLECTIONS

What stands out for you about your *What If?* musings from applying a *better endings* lens? Are there buried wishes showing up in your *What If* re-visioning stories? Journal in the pages provided below and/or in your Better Endings Journal about what lessons you will take away from exploring your *What If?* potentials.

How might the different outcomes you can envision from these *'what would have happened if'* scenarios you are journaling about have mattered in the bigger picture of your life goals and values? What stands out as basically immutable about your life, regardless of circumstances?

Would you still be basically the person you are now, or how might your life be changed? Would you be happier? How so, or why not?

How can you use your reflections about *What Ifs* from your past to better approach current or future choices? What specific steps could you set into motion now so you might finally realize something you feel you have missed in your life due to twists of choice or fortune from your past?

CLOSING THOUGHTS

I find musing on *What If?* scenarios to be a very energizing, playful exercise. It reminds me of how children create imaginative *What If?* scenarios when they play with one another. When I was a child I had a great childhood friend, Karin. We would play at being cowboys and Indians sometimes, or World War II soldiers, or Star Trek characters on daring Enterprise adventures, or even wild horses! When playing with dolls we would set up huge mansions made of golden-book walls on my family's ping-pong table, and for days or sometimes weeks at a time we would create entire lifetimes for our favorite characters.

Children's play worlds may not consciously be about creating *better endings* scenarios based on their own lives, but unconsciously they could be. I was always the Indian, never the cowboy; then later in life I became a Native American anthropologist.

I was Ken and never Barbie, always a tomboy, and I grew up to be a very independently minded woman who sometimes jokes that my casual wardrobe comes from my Ken doll's case. Why did we create specific locations and careers for our characters? My Ken was usually a scientist or a teacher when not engaged with international intrigue as a military officer or spy.

In retrospect, in child play we felt free to explore and express different archetypal facets of our developing selves, while also we could try on for size various *better ending* scenarios for our lives!

Can you approach your adult *What If?* reflections with the same flexibility and energy of playful abandon that you enjoyed as a child?

Well then, who are you now? Who do you want to be, when you "grow up?"

Better Endings Story Seed

What If?

1. Make a list of 3-5 situations from your past that could benefit from *What If?* reflections.

_____

_____

_____

_____

_____

2. Circle one or more of the *What If?* topics from your list. In the pages provided below, and/or in your Better Endings Journal, play with these situations. What might have turned out differently and how might that have affected the person you would have become? You could explore multiple scenarios to re-vision alternative outcomes for the same situation.

My Reflections

Reflect about what you have learned about yourself from envisioning *What If?* scenarios. What changes of direction has your life taken from these decision points that you are grateful for? What elements of what might have been would you still like to realize? How will you fulfill these goals?

Chapter 12

From Lesions to Lessons

Our physical, emotional, and mental health influence our sense of well-being throughout our lives. Most of the time for most people, health is relatively manageable. Aging may bring extra challenges along with hereditary genetic conditions. Exposure to viral infections can bring temporary illness, or worse, as our recent global pandemic has punctuated. Emotional upsets or brain chemistry imbalances might lead to depression or other psychological maladies, and physical accidents by which we break a bone or even become paraplegic could affect our lives either in the short term or forevermore.

The principle of Better Endings can be of immense value when reflecting on matters of your health and wellbeing. Healing is itself a *better ending* for an illness or for a difficult physical or emotional trauma, but how we engage with and understand a health condition and its aftermath—whether it resolves to wellness, or not—may matter even more.

We can regard any illness or physical challenge as a blessing that brings vital life lessons and a greater potential capacity to give and receive love.

Christopher Reeve is remembered as an archetype for transforming a health calamity into a gift, or at least a mixed blessing, however tragic. Paralyzed from the neck down after being thrown from a horse, he never fully recovered physically. Yet, Christopher Reeve maintained a strong, optimistic attitude: he never stopped striving to overcome his condition; he never stepped down from opportunities to inspire and encourage others; he never stopped expressing his love and gratitude for his wife and family and life itself; he never stopped thriving.

Many who face severe illnesses such as cancer or MS similarly not only pursue their most helpful treatments but they also strive to live in the best way possible with their conditions, accepting that through their ordeals they may have much to gain in terms of greater wisdom and love. This sort of *better endings* attitude can prevent an illness from afflicting the most elemental, essential attribute of our human nature: our eternal spirit.

My Turn: Never Again!

A few years back I encountered traumatic circumstances while traveling on a one-month road trip. I rented a house in New York state that turned out to be infested with all manner of parasitic bugs! Bed bugs, bird mites, even body lice... all attacked me within days until my body was riddled with lesions from head to foot. I had with me my dear dog companion Sophie, and she too became afflicted by some of these pests.

It was awful. I laundered repeatedly, to no avail. A pest removal person killed bed bugs in one room and declared the other rooms clear; how wrong he was! Ultimately after a 3AM trip to the emergency room for a near anaphylactic shock reaction to a bite, and to a vet without full resolution, about one week in I decided to make a break for freedom. After detailing my car and washing Sophie one more time, I abandoned my belongings and all clothing but for a new set I had saved in a plastic bag. I fled with Sophie to a bed and breakfast where the compassionate owner, who was an Emergency Medical Technician, took it upon herself to help me and Sophie to recover and rid ourselves and our car of the terrible scourge that had beset us. Because this landlady could have lost her B&B license for harboring someone potentially bringing in pests to the home, she required me to maintain silence in public about my condition. I felt isolated and outcast, shamed as a social pariah.

It took six weeks that felt much longer and well over six thousand dollars for me to treat the infestation and heal the bodily lesions I and my dog endured. The bugs persisted throughout most of that time despite all I was doing to cleanse and heal; this meant more bites, more visits to urgent cares and vets and dermatologists along with twice daily medicinal showers, vigorous vacuuming, daily change of bedding and renewal of deeply laundered clothes, more car treatments and room bombings, and very little sleep. Literally I would sit down on a freshly laundered white sheet only to see little black mites surfacing within minutes. Eventually I abandoned even the B&B bed, sleeping with Sophie in our small bathroom on a tile floor, taping the bottom threshold of the door with duct tape to prevent critters from creeping in. Upon morning I would count from the tape how many tiny bugs had tried to breach the threshold.

Throughout this long affliction I felt reduced in spirit and body to the point that I was not at all certain I would survive. I well remember one night in particular when, after nearly fainting from yet another mid-back bite with the associated dizziness that could mean an anaphylactic reaction in process, I was unwilling to go to yet another urgent care or to wake my sister 45 minutes away or my hostess. So instead, I wrote on a napkin whom to send my dog to for care and a list of who to invite to my funeral; I left this on the bureau before finally succumbing to a fitful sleep.

So, where is the *better endings* angle on my and Sophie's traumatic bug scourge? Well, every morning—once I had made it through another gruesome night—offered me a fresh opportunity to confront the problem and try to assuage the injuries and find healing. I sought out and relied upon inner spiritual guidance more than ever before, moment to moment, and it helped! I felt guided to the smallest decisions, like where to find cheap clothes and food rations on the miniscule budget I had left, how to get the car detailed without reinfesting it later, when to leave Sophie at doggie daycare while cleansing self and car and room yet one more time, what next bomb to buy at Walmart, how to use a lint roller to capture samples of the mites to show a doctor, or which over the counter medicines to use in addition to the prescribed salves.

Slowly, gradually, after bolting to drive myself and my dog home early to Colorado while still beset with festering wounds, and still after delivering Sophie to safety with friends in Colorado while I remained in isolation for a final dermatology appointment and car detailing so I could be medically declared free to fly back to New York to attend my ninety-year old mother's birthday, the body healed and all pests were eliminated. By then I had so succumbed to paranoia that during the final trip to my mother's celebration I honestly no longer could tell whether I was still beset, or not. By then I carried my minimal belongings in plastic lawn bags into a hotel, which I also had worn over my legs and torso in the car en route to the airport. I was fully reduced to what felt like the level of a bug myself.

Gratefully, my family and later colleagues and housemates and friends at home helped me regain my humanity and sense of trust. But this was an ordeal that affected me so deeply that I know it has changed the fabric of who I am forever more.

I could happily fantasize a *better endings* scenario in which I avoided this terrible experience altogether. But honestly, I would not be in some measure the person I am grateful to be today had this experience never occurred. So, I would not rewrite altogether what happened but will always remember the kindness of strangers, family, colleagues, friends, my still beloved dog companion Sophie and my loving inner guidance for the help I received and the life lessons that I learned along the way.

MY REFLECTIONS

In retrospect I gained in humility and fortitude from surviving this horrific ordeal. While I am now exceedingly careful to avoid bug infestations of any sort, I feel fortunate and thankful every day to be alive and free of the scourge. These are *better endings* results: lessons learned through a difficult process of confronting a challenging health condition.

Even if had I not survived, I would say the experience would have had some positive value. Day to day I felt surrounded by love and caring, from the hostess who helped me at the bed and breakfast, from doctors, from my dear Sophie who went through this ordeal with me and is still by my side, from my generous sister who lived nearby, and inwardly I felt the ongoing companionship and guidance of divine love.

I am in some ways a different and a better person because of this difficult ordeal. I feel humbled. I can appreciate how people feel when their health is jeopardized, or when their belongings are stripped away. I feel more resilient and resourceful knowing I survived a harrowing threat, alone with my dog some 2400 miles away from our home. At the same time, I feel more reserved in public at some deep inner level ever since, because this was such an alienating experience that I went through humanly alone. This feeling of aloneness is at times a comfort, though it is also something I try to tend to by reaching out to stay better connected with my family and close friends.

YOUR TURN

Have you experienced a health-related ordeal which might benefit from the vantage point of a *better-endings* lens? This could be an illness or a psychological condition or any situation you have found deeply challenging from a health perspective.

Using the prompts in the Better Endings Story Seed section at the end of this chapter, tell your story (one or more) in the pages provided below, and/or in your Better Endings Journal. What happened? Were there choices involved and how did you make these choices? What helpful persons or agencies did you utilize and how were you led to them? How did you feel as you underwent the sequence of significant events that marked this difficult time in your life? If you are still living through this ordeal or its aftermath, account for where you are at today and what are your hopes for the future.

Describe your experience fully. Remember to allow yourself to re-vision your feelings as well as events. Make sure to include a *better endings* focus: what positive life lessons do you take away from this experience? How are you a better person from before and after confronting your health challenge? What are you grateful for? How will you go forward from here with greater awareness and love?

YOUR REFLECTIONS

After writing your story (one or more), reflect in the pages provided below and/or in your Better Endings Journal about what you will take away from re-visioning one or more of your health-related challenges. What insights have you gained that you might like to share with others for their benefit?

What life lessons have you learned, or if this is an ongoing situation, what are you in the process of learning from your ordeal?

CLOSING THOUGHTS

Health matters, not only in terms of our physical, psychological, and emotional wellbeing. Our journey through conditions or situations that impact our health imparts vital lessons that can affect the trajectory of our lives forever after.

How have your health-related experiences affected the person you are today? What vital life lessons have they helped you to apply to your life going forward?

Better Endings Story Seed

From Lesions to Lessons

1. Make a list of 3-5 health related challenges you have had to confront in your life.

   _____

   _____

   _____

   _____

   _____

2. Circle one (or more) of the challenges you have listed and compose a full account of your experience, from your present day perspective, in the pages provided below, and/ or in your Better Endings Journal. Describe what happened, what resources you had available to understand and treat the condition, and what resulted. Include a *better endings* focus by identifying positive outcomes or life lessons you have taken away from your experience.

My Reflections

What have you learned from facing difficult health challenges? In what ways has this affected the person you are today, positively and/or negatively?

_____

_____

_____

_____

_____

_____

_____

_____

_____

_____

_____

_____

_____

_____

_____

_____

_____

_____

_____

Chapter 13

Second Chances

D o you sometimes wish that in the best of all possible worlds you would get a second chance with respect to some significant, life altering decision or relationship from your past? Second chances is a common *better endings* theme, found in many a work of fiction or film. How might you apply your *better endings* creative license to write in a second chance for yourself in some important chapter from your life story?

Let's play in our creative sandbox of the imagination with this one. Here is your chance to reflect on that great enigma afterthought: "If Only." *If only* I had been more patient or more kind; *If only* I had listened better or had recognized that golden opportunity; or, *If only* I didn't throw away that winning lottery ticket! Such wistful thinking can plague us long after a situation has passed for better or worse, as only time has told.

MY TURN

When I was twenty-one, during the summer following my junior year in college, I worked as an usher at a performing arts center in my hometown. As an English major in college and an avid journal writer, I had for several years harbored a dream of moving to New York City to become an author. I imagined sitting nightly in candlelit coffeehouses with live folk music in the City: the ideal setting for composing poetry and stories to fulfill my passion for creative expression.

One Saturday morning that summer, after a symphony performance for which I had ushered the night before, I received a surprising call from an older friend who was herself a talented local director and actress, Donna. Donna called to tell me that the famous conductor of the visiting symphony and his wife were looking to hire a nanny for their two boys. They lived in New York City and Donna, knowing of my ambitions, recommended me to them. They were leaving Monday morning to return to the City so they needed me to decide right away, and they would bring me home with them.

What an opportunity! This would certainly be a life changing leap into a future I could hardly imagine. It would mean forgoing graduate school at least temporarily to pursue a writing career while serving as a nanny for a world-renowned celebrity. Oddly enough, one of my aunts was herself a nanny for another well-known celebrity.

Here was my big, once in a lifetime chance to launch a dynamic career; with a place to live, a job, and a salary in the Big Apple. I wanted to accept. But as much as I was excited by and grateful for the offer, that Sunday morning I called Donna and told her to let the conductor know I was declining the offer. I simply could not make such a huge break at that time. I told myself I had no genuine desire to be a nanny.

I wanted to finish my degree, after all, safe and secure in my familiar surroundings. Privately I also felt deflated by the opportunity; my big city dreams were exposed as a pipe dream fantasy, never to be fulfilled.

So now, let me entertain a *better endings* re-visioning of what might-have-happened *If only* I had accepted this Godsend sort of offer.

For my "second chances" story, I will use first person pronouns and write in the historical present tense, as I encourage you to use also in your second-chances story. This lets you re-vision your experience with a sense of immediacy, so you can imaginatively relive—and playfully rescript—your memories.

My Life in the City

I accept the offer to leave with the conductor's family to serve as a nanny in NYC. I understand this means I need to leave college and my family and friends to embark on this leap of faith. I pack my one college trunk and show up on that fateful Monday morning at the performing arts center parking lot, ready to be whisked away to the Big Apple, to follow my destiny.

I enjoy being a nanny much more than I thought I would. The boys in my charge are talented in their own rights and I encourage them to bloom as young musicians at a performing arts school in the City. I transfer to Columbia University for my senior year in college. I complete my English degree, then I go on still at Columbia to earn a Master of Fine Arts in writing and journalism.

I frequent my favorite coffeehouse, both alone and with my new college friends. I write and eventually publish short stories, screenplays, science fiction, and poetry. I love the folk music scene and Broadway plays. Professionally, first I take a job at The New Yorker as a proofreader for a few years, and later I become an editor for a major book publisher.

As an editor I meet a literary agent at a writers' conference in southern California—the same marvelous agent I am a client for in my parallel life [now]. She encourages me to write a blog which I later draw on as the foundation for a self-discovery based, personal growth and creative journaling book: *Better Endings*.

MY REFLECTIONS

Funny. When I trace a thread forward from my re-visioned second chance, I end up near to where I am anyways today, in many respects. I am a writer, and oddly enough in my semi-retirement life I also serve as an editor for a local publishing company. Had I taken the nanny job in New York City, yet eventually had also still written this book, maybe I might have come to envision the life I have actually lived—since turning the nanny offer down—as my imagined 'second chance' story! Perhaps parallel worlds are not necessarily so far apart, after all!

YOUR TURN

Is there a significant, life changing decision you have made over the course of your life; some opportunity you turned down or overlooked for its potential significance at the time? Perhaps it was a relationship choice which you still often wonder about, or a golden career opportunity that seemed too risky or too good at the time to be true? What might have come about for you *if only* you had chosen differently and followed that alternative pathway forward?

Based on the Better Endings Story Seed prompts at the end of this chapter, choose one or more of your roads not taken to re-vision as 'second chances.' Tell your story in the pages provided below and/ or in your Better Endings Journal using first person, historical present tense; imagining yourself back in the time when you were faced with that key decision. Write in first person as if this time you have chosen differently at this critical juncture. What then imaginatively transpires in your life from this point forward?

Explore this alternative life path freely. Aim to sustain your 'second chance' story up to what your life might look like today had you chosen differently at that would-be turning point.

YOUR REFLECTIONS

What have you revealed about yourself from re-visioning what could have followed from making a different decision in your life?

Do you arrive back at somewhere near to where you are today, as I did in my sample musing? Or rather, does your reconstruction of how things might have been lead you to a very different setting and lifestyle than you are living now?

What stays the same and what differs in your two alternative, 'parallel' lives? Does this reveal somewhat your core values or goals, regardless of external circumstances?

If your second chances story brings up some *better endings* ambition that you still wish you could fulfill in your life today, how can you still pursue that ideal?

CLOSING THOUGHTS

We all face significant decisions now and again: choices that could alter the entire trajectory of our lives from that point forward.

This chapter's Second Chances thought experiment allows you, at least whimsically, to peek at a possible parallel reality, or 'alti-verse.'

Modern physicists theorize that we may in fact occupy a multiverse, so that each possibility arising from every decision we have ever made is playing out in some dimension parallel to the life we are living here and now. Does creative re-visioning offer us at least a thought bridge then, between dimensions?

Bringing the principle of Better Endings with us on a thought experiment about Second Chances allows us to ask meaningful questions about where we are in our lives today compared with where we might have been if we had chosen differently. The fact that we can muse about how our life could have unfolded differently from having made a different significant choice along the way, shows that through exercising our imagination we can explore and thereby experience all our potentials, whether outwardly realized or not.

Is there a ripple effect when you use your imagination to peek in on some alternate, unchosen pathway? How might you use the insights you have gained from your Second Chances reflections to make *better endings* choices going forward?

Better Endings Story Seed

Second Chances

1. Make a list of 3-5 opportunities in your past that would have led you in a different direction with respect to your career, relationships, or travel; but that you declined.

_____

_____

_____

_____

_____

2. Circle one or more of the decision points listed above. In the pages provided below and/or in your Better Endings Journal tell forth a 'second chance' scenario in which you have taken the path that you declined. Use 1st person ('I') point of view and present tense (as if now) to tell your second-chance story, as if you had taken that path. Carry your re-visioned story forward to present time.

My Reflections

Reflect in the pages provided below and/or in your Better Endings Journal about your second-chances story. Are you happy you declined the past opportunity because in retrospect you were following your best intuition, or do you wonder whether your life might have been better in certain respects *if only* you had chosen or acted differently? What might you do about that, now?

Chapter 14

Loss and Recovery

Another topic worthy of our consideration regarding how to facilitate *better endings* is loss. Loss can affect anyone deeply, whether from natural disasters or accidents, theft, health issues, changes in relationships, refugee relocation, or any impactful situation that results in loss of property, impaired safety and security, or losses of the heart. Recovery from loss itself might be thought of as a natural form of *better ending*, but how one recovers, and whether recovery is even emotionally or physically possible at all, may affect the quality of someone's life forever after.

There are two kinds of stories people commonly tell about their experience of loss and recovery. One story focuses on the recovery process itself and what remains or develops anew despite their loss of loved ones, property or life conditions. The other narrative centers around unrecoverable losses of the heart and the survivor's desire to bring meaning or value to that loss. Finding meaning or value after a loss is vital for our capacity to go forward.

I have known people who lost their homes and property, some also their pets, to major fires that broke out several years ago while I was living in Colorado. One, a college student, told me that when her parents went back to examine the rubble of what had been their family home since her birth, they found only one remnant item in the ashes: an unframed paper photograph of their daughter, the student, when she was just a baby. Another person, a therapist friend who lost her house and two pets and all her property to a fire, showed me a picture of a ceremonial sweat lodge she had constructed out of dried tree limbs that remained unscathed although it was right in the path of the fire that consumed her home not twenty yards away, along with all surrounding trees and other brush near the flimsy structure.

'Why me?' people ask themselves. 'Why did I survive when others did not?' Or 'Why was my house taken while others were spared?'

We look for meaning in these crises, something to take away from the traumatic events that we can use to rebuild, to recover. We reach to find meaning ever more so when the loss is of the heart; when we lose a loved one, especially due to an unexpected, tragic event. That is the sort of story I will share, about the loss of my dear dog companion, Ellie.

MY TURN: Ellie, The Dog That Ran

Ellie was a sweet, timid, "one person" (me) sort of dog, an orange Rhodesian ridgeback/ boxer mix that I brought home when she was a puppy from a humane society. Ellie grew up with my other, older dog Skyway, who passed away naturally of old age on the very day a vet informed me that Ellie's tendency to grow mass cell tumors was likely to kill her within six months. That did not occur, because a friend who owned a vitamin store referred me to a doctor in Conifer,

CO, who had developed a treatment called molecular cell therapy that could cure cancerous tumors in dogs. Four years and many daily subcutaneous treatments later Ellie, at eleven, was still doing fine and she had already lived to a normal life expectancy for her size and breed.

One summer day I brought Ellie with me to visit with a friend and her daughter near Denver (I lived in Colorado Springs). I left Ellie in the wood-fenced back yard behind my friend's house along with my friend's sheltie, while we went for breakfast. I visually inspected the back yard fence and gate before leaving, and everything seemed safe for Ellie even though I knew she would be stressed by being with a playful dog she had not met before.

A couple hours later my friends and I returned from breakfast; Ellie was not in the yard! A neighbor reported she had jumped up against the fence gate at the side of the house and it had opened, so Ellie had run out looking for me. The neighbors did not recognize her and dear Ellie would have been too timid to let anyone near her anyway. Apparently, someone did approach Ellie and she bolted down the unfamiliar suburban street, in a busy neighborhood area interspersed with green belts between the blocks.

Probably looking for me frantically, Ellie never found her way back to my friend's house or to me. My friend and her daughter helped me for days to search the area, put up signs, talk to all the neighbors, walk the greenways. For two and a half months I searched for Ellie at all the shelters near and far from my friend's neighborhood, posted on Craigslist and in classified newspaper ads. I dreamed about her whereabouts and tried to follow my inner guidance; I received several reports via texts responding to my ads of what seemed like possible sightings, but by the time I would arrive to search, Ellie was nowhere to be found.

I felt so terrible about Ellie being gone and lost. Such a dear and timid dog, and in treatment for her tumor condition; I could only imagine the most horrible possibilities of what might have befallen her. She was unlikely to warm up to strangers; I feared she might have sought refuge under greenway brush only to be attacked by some coyote or other predator at night.

Anyway, I never did find Ellie. Well-meaning friends assured me they felt she had been taken in my someone who cared for her themselves, but such pie-in-the-sky suggestions were never truly consoling to me.

All I could do, which I did, to try to at least bring some closure to my grief over Ellie's loss, was to hold a ceremony for her with two friends. Near to where I thought Ellie might have run, I buried some of her favorite toys, treats, and belongings. I read spiritual passages and gave her a memorial service.

Better endings? Six months later when I could finally bear to admit to myself that Ellie was not to be found, I adopted a new little puppy, a sweet little Shorkie (Shih Tzu/ Yorkie), Sophie, who as a very dear companion is still with me, at her eleventh birthday today as I write this journal entry.

Because of Ellie's demise, I had Sophie chipped when she was a puppy and I renew her location chip's registry every year, so if by any rare chance she would become separated from me, a vet or humane society staff would contact me.

Over the years since I lost Ellie I have tried to rescue several obviously lost dogs, either contacting their owners if they had information on their collar or taking them to the humane society so their owners could find them there. I think of Ellie every time, of course. I hope this has brought some *better endings* to at least these other dogs and their owners.

MY REFLECTIONS

A loss of the heart, such as my loss of dear Ellie, can never be repaired. I feel as deeply about her loss as a parent must feel about the tragic loss of their child. When this occurs, a parent often speaks out, starts a research fund, or even starts a movement to prevent the same sort of tragedy that beset their family from afflicting the lives of others.

Anti-gun movements, Moms Against Drunk Drivers, and youth diabetes funds started by grieving parents all share a common ground: these parents or survivors of tragedy whose loved ones have perished seek to 'bring meaning' to the life, and death, of their dearly beloved. They aim to bring lessons from their tragic loss forward to serve others, as they know that their loved one would want them to do, even from the beyond.

YOUR TURN

Clearly this chapter's theme of Loss and Recovery is not a fun topic, particularly if it recalls for you a tragic loss. Remember as we have considered from the start how not all *better endings* are happy ones; our purpose here is not about creating fantasies to deny our pain or to hide from our necessary grief.

Better endings in the case of irretrievable loss may be reached mainly from telling your story, to reflect upon whatever meaning or lessons you carry forward with you, as you recover what you can and bring the value forward.

Some of the losses you may wish to re-vision did result in recovery; and that is great! It can still be helpful to re-vision the times when your loss occurred; to review how the recovery came about and how it has influenced you and your loved ones since.

Using the Better Endings Story Seed prompts at the end of this chapter, list some losses you have experienced or if you know of someone else's deep loss you could include that too. Choose one or more of these situations involving loss and in the pages provided below, and/or in your Better Endings Journal, recount what happened. Bring each story through to what has felt like closure for you, if that is yet possible at all, or to where you are at currently in relation to the situation.

Remember to bring a *better endings* lens to telling your story of loss and recovery. This could involve accounting for the meaning or value of the experience in relation to aftermath developments in your life, or it might simply mean remembering and expressing with gratitude and love how dear a person or pet that you have lost was and still is, to you and to others.

YOUR REFLECTIONS

Write in the pages provided below and/or in your Better Endings Journal about the value of remembering the situations of loss you have re-visioned. If this involved a loss of the heart that is truly unrecoverable, acknowledge your feelings about your loss and reflect on the meaning or value of this loved one or of the experience itself in your life.

If there was a recovery from your loss that you or others were able to bring about, you can reflect upon the full impact of that situation and how it has affected you and your loved ones.

Are there lessons to be learned that you would share in your story to help others prevent or prepare for what you and your loved ones have had to endure? Bring a *better-endings* perspective to your reflections by acknowledging how you and your loved ones have been able to move forward, even with greater purpose or love, since your loss.

CLOSING THOUGHTS

Gay Becker, an anthropologist, wrote a book called *Disrupted Lives* based on her extensive interviews with people who had suffered tragic loss either due to natural disasters or as wartime refugees. She found that a common denominator running through their stories was how these survivors of tragedy always attributed great meaning and value to their experiences of loss as they remembered all they and their loved ones had endured. If that horrendous hurricane had not occurred, stripping away their lifelong home with all their belongings, they might say, they would have never made that life changing Big Move from which they and their family later benefitted. Or, though their loss of the heart was irreparable, they have learned so much even in their grief and would live the rest of their lives in such manner as to do honor to those departed.

We may find much to be grateful for, or at least to bring forward, in remembering our loss.

Better Endings Story Seed

Loss and Recovery

1. Make a list of 3-5 situations from your life that have involved tragic or irretrievable loss and/or, if relevant, recovery. You may wish to include situations you know about from friends or family members.

2. Describe one or more of your situations of loss in the pages provided below and/or in your Better Endings Journal. Write about how the experience unfolded and about how or whether you have yet achieved closure.

My Reflections

Either in your account of the situations of loss you have described or after writing out your story, add a *better endings* perspective by reflecting about what meaning or value you take forward from your experience that adds to your sense of recovery or closure. What may never be the same? What can or have you done to honor your lost loved ones, to move forward in your life as they would want you to, or to pass along your greatest lessons learned?

Chapter 15

At a Crossroads: Alternative Futures

Turning Points, Big Moves, What Ifs, Silver Linings, Lesions to Lessons, Second Chances, Loss and Recovery: all these excursions with your Better Endings Journal re-visioning have allowed you to take a step or two back in time, to gain perspective and gather thrust to propel you forth into better tomorrows, ripe with greater self-awareness and purpose. 'Live, and learn!' could be our mantra for *better endings* creative re-visioning.

Next then, let's turn the *better endings* lens around to shine our light not to illuminate the past but ahead from where we are: into the future!

Imagine a postcard with a picture that represents where you are standing in your life right now, on which you place an arrow that says, 'I am here!'

Where are you? Now then, conceive of wherever you are now as at a significant crossroads, opening to an ever more bounteous future. What new directions can you foresee that are attainable to you from here? Like Robert Frost's poetic image of paths diverging in a woods, would you rather stay the course you are traveling upon or step over to a path forward you may have considered before but have not taken? What are your goals or aspirations, your *better endings* intentions for wending your life path forward from here?

A helpful tool for future prospecting—that is, for envisioning desirable future conditions—is to journal about or imagine and artistically represent not one but several alternate "futurescapes." From where you stand in your life today, your future exists as an array of possibilities fanning out in relatively unlimited directions, determined mainly by your current intentions, choices, and actions.

Flexibility is your golden key for unlocking exciting new pathways to fulfill your *better endings* future life path. That is why when you set out to envision your most desirable, achievable future, it is helpful to imagine a set of several possible scenarios.

My Turn

[Initially composed, March 2020]: My 'I am Here' postcard shows an aerial view of two kayakers, paddling along on a river about to flow into the mouth of a Great Lake. Although I am at a reasonably comfortable place as I write, I often consider what might be possible beyond the bends ahead in my life's journey.

I can envision several alternate possible futurescapes: landscapes, so to speak, of my possible future. Some of these are of the wild fantasy type, others more practical and realistic.

> *Futurescape #1 (fantasy based)*: I am sitting against a driftwood log outside my cottage in the West of Ireland. I live in a small community of retired seniors, most of them artists or writers. We occupy a half ring of cottages just up from a secluded,

silvery beach. We have a common house for social gatherings and community cooking, but we also enjoy our freedom and privacy. There are unicorns that play on the beach by day, and Pegasus horses shimmer over the sea as they traverse to nearby isles.

Future Scape #2: I have survived. The global pandemic scare has finally lifted, as doctors around the world collaborated to create an effective and readily available vaccine more quickly than anyone would have thought possible. After being mainly self-cloistered with my pets for nearly a year, now I want to spread my wings, and fly!

I see myself renting a medium-sized camper RV, packing needed supplies, and heading out cross-country with my beloved dog and cat for at least a full month's road trip. There are a few places I travel to, meeting up with and sharing legs of the trip with a few close friends. There are some favorite places from my past that we visit: Zuni, Sedona, and the Colorado mountains; but I remain open to driving in whatever new directions my heart leads me to explore, day by day.

When I return home with my pets, I begin planning for yet another move. In this still fantasy yet more practical scenario, the new home I move to is like Frodo's earth home in a Hobbit shire with roads, both metaphorically and for real, leading off in all directions from the secluded village. I grow my own veggies in a communal garden which I share within a collaborative yet privacy-permitting, intentional community. Laughter and art fill the air in this place, as the residents of this shire are mainly artists, musicians, spiritual practitioners of diverse faiths, animal lovers, and caregivers. This is a conscious community that I have gravitated to based on my ideal values.

Future Scape #3: When I return home from my six-week camping trip, within a year I sell my home and move again. I find an affordable, well kept, small lakeside or canal side cottage, nearer than before to one of my dear sisters and a longtime friend. I have my dear pets with me and the kayaks are racked outside by my own dock. I have a labyrinth installed inside a gazebo enclosed with plexiglass, so I can walk the labyrinth year-round in open view of the lake. This new home is my haven for reading and writing, for long walks and daily contemplation, and for sharing with family and friends. A dear friend has also moved into a house on farmland nearby.

Future Scape #4: I stay put and grow to love my lakeside village retirement home, more and more. I add a kayak that fits inside my car to explore a network of lakes and canals in the region. I continue with my writing and local spiritual activities, and I join or help to form a dynamic new area reading circle. Over time I explore far and wide from my home base, taking my pets with me as I am able. Eventually I move again, into a more permanent retirement community, when I find exactly what I am looking for: one that allows a companionable yet independent lifestyle. A couple of friends also buy an independent cottage there.

My sister and I also rent a cabin half-distant between us every summer for a month, and otherwise we visit frequently. Eventually I also travel globally every year, with my sisters and brother or sometimes with a good friend or two. We visit Ireland and several other countries mainly in Europe, India, and Nepal.

MY REFLECTIONS

In reviewing common denominators that run across my projected alternate futurescapes, I find several common themes: verdant, near-waterside environments; travel opportunities that include my pets, friends and siblings; reading groups; a peaceful environment for writing and contemplation; close friends and family nearby; and a dynamic community spirit.

Which or as much of these or other specific futurescapes I may eventually manifest does not matter so much, as now I am aware of these core elements that matter most. After envisioning these multiple futures, from the most fantastic to very practical possibilities, I feel more relaxed, with a greater sense of freedom. With an expanded vision of what is possible down the road, I feel less constrained, even by the current pandemic conditions.

Addendum, two years later (March 2022): I did move again, and when I re-read especially Futurescape#2 that I envisioned almost exactly two years ago, I am struck by how closely my move has matched my futurescape projection.

My move just over a year ago was to a locale that is walking distance from a river that flows into an actual Great Lake! I live nearer to my sister and fifteen minutes from my best high school friend and her husband, back in my familiar hometown; I have proverbially returned Home. The alternate futurescape journaling I used two years ago to imaginatively look ahead truly did serve like a crystal ball of sorts, but how? It helped me reveal to myself my deepest future yearnings, which have unconsciously guided me forward.

YOUR TURN

Using the journaling prompts in the Better Endings Journal Seed at the end of this chapter, you will be invited to look ahead several months and/or up to several years from today, to envision where you might be in that future "Now." As the one constant in life is change, what sorts of changes would you like your ideal future to hold in store for you? Are you staying in the place and home you love but making tweaks to improve your life conditions? Or do you make a big break to finally take that long distance trip or to move to or retire to a place of your dreams?

Remember, you are the author, editor, and the main heroic character in your own life story, no less so for your future adventures!

With the Better Endings Story Seed prompts as your guide and your journaling in the pages provided below and/or in Better Endings Journal as a timeship, first take yourself on a voyage to a fantastical future of your heart's desire. Place yourself in some desirable fantasy future and view your life from this point of view. Journal just one page from a 1st person, present tense point of view. There are no limits for this fantasy based alternate futurescape, so spread your wings of imagination and let yourself land in some far-flung future of your wildest desire!

After journaling your first, fantasy-based future scenario, you will be invited to turn to a new page in your journal and envision a different futurescape, this time one more practical but that still expresses ideal future desires and values. Continue to write in 1st person, present tense as if you are living Now in that desirable future. This can feel like you are writing from your future self to your present self, describing your new life conditions and environment.

It is important with this alternate futurescape journaling tool for you to envision and explore multiple future scenarios, not just one or two. Imagine at least three to five possible futures, allowing yourself to include the best features of the places and qualities you would love to actualize one way or another in your future.

YOUR REFLECTIONS

After you feel satisfied that you have prospected and 'mined' a meaningful range of your future potentials and desires, still using the journaling prompts from the Better Endings Story Seed section below, go back and review your multiple future scenarios. What common elements are shared across the future scenarios you have projected? How do they differ? Reflect on how these shared elements illumine what you are really after with your lifelong ambitions, your deepest felt future ideals.

Which of your most core future values and conditions are available to you where you are at currently, with just some basic adjustments? Which are attainable with some significant but practical changes? How might you begin now or in the near foreseeable future to move in a direction that propels you to actualize the *better ending* future of your innermost desire?

CLOSING THOUGHTS

Imagining and journaling about multiple future potentials is a form of future prospecting, like panning for gold. The Future is never fixed or set in stone. It is a dynamic array, a branching network of possible and somewhat foreseeable future conditions. Which future you create as you move along in your life's journey depends in large part on the flexibility of the vision you hold and the choices you are ready to make in the present. You have the creative license to actualize your *better endings* future, by following truly your heart's desire.

The key benefit of envisioning multiple 'futurescapes' is that after you visualize several desirable scenarios, you can review them to discover not only how they differ but more importantly, what they have in common. These common denominator ideals reflect your core values and reveal some of the deepest future desires of your heart.

Identifying your core values and exposing your unconscious as well as conscious yearnings sets you on a clearer path to actualize your ambitions, to Live Your Dream!

Better Endings Story Seed

At a Crossroads: Alternative Futures

1. Make a list of 5-7 alternate future scenarios.

----

2. Select three or more of the most desirable future scenarios you have listed. Starting with a fantasy-based future scenario, write no more than one page in the pages provided below, and/or in your Better Endings Journal, using 1st person, present tense, as if you are living in this improbable, desirable 'alternate futurescape.' Then compose two or more additional one-page projections of more practical yet still desirable futures, still in 1st person, present tense.

My Reflections

Reflect about what your alternate futurescapes have in common. Identify the future qualities and values most important to you in these alternate futures. What can you do to bring about the core values of your desired *better endings* future?

Chapter 16

Your Better Endings Legacy

Your legacy is what you will leave behind as enrichment for your loved ones and others to remember you by and potentially for them to grow by and learn from in their own lives. A life legacy could take many forms. Some write autobiographical memoirs or compile rich photo journals to leave for their family. Some secure financial reserves that will transfer to their loved ones after their departure.

Building a legacy need not be primarily for seniors or elderly people. No matter what stage or chapter you are at in your life story today, you are always shaping your legacy.

A personal growth and development tool many have used to explore their own legacy involves writing your own obituary. I like the idea of composing not an obituary but a eulogy to illuminate your *better endings* legacy. A eulogy is a speech or essay that celebrates a life well lived. It might highlight all that someone has accomplished, their gifts and talents, and how that person has been of service to their family and community.

I had a dear friend who passed recently who was herself an author. Having several months to prepare for her transition from a terminal illness, my friend benefitted from writing her own eulogy, which was a combination of what she would want said of her and what some of her friends had written about her by her request. She emphasized in her eulogy, in a humorous tone, not only some elements of her colorful life history and of her proudest accomplishments, but she also wrote about her deepest aspirations and the values she had lived by. This eulogy, published after her departure instead of a normal obituary and included on the program for her memorial service, portrayed and celebrated the very spirit of my friend. I am glad that she left this for those of us grieving her loss to better know and remember her by.

You might compose your eulogy either from the point of view of the present or else, as a *better endings* scenario, from the perspective of a future time when you would feel you have fulfilled your major life goals or ambitions.

So, I will invite you with the Better Endings Story Seed prompts below to journal two versions of your own eulogy: first, from the immediate present (because, who knows, right?); and then second, from the point of view of a future time by which you will have even more greatly fulfilled the legacy you would most wish to share with your loved ones.

If I were to pass beyond today, I would want to be remembered for what I have so far accomplished and for my relations and gratitude now.

When I envision a future time of passing, I can project elements I hope to have accomplished by then, which I can work toward from now to fulfill.

MY TURN

My current eulogy is a celebration of what I have accomplished in my life to date, and it acknowledges my love and gratitude for my family, my pet companions, and my dear friends. I do not feel the need to model that one for you here.

My second, *better endings* eulogy looks ahead to my completing some projects I feel passionate about and hope to complete in the future; and it is also about further developing my understanding of truth and expanding my deepest service capacity. One brief excerpt from my future oriented eulogy could include:

> Linda published a series of books offering an inspirational, personal development approach of "self-discovery journaling," as well as serving over forty-five years as a professor of anthropology. She maintained an active service role with her spiritual community, dedicating much of her life to understanding spiritual principles and delving ever more deeply into the nature of life and the cosmos. She graduated unto her further unfolding adventures as Soul with a grateful smile.

MY REFLECTIONS

Writing a future oriented eulogy helps me recognize my core values and recommit to some of my deepest lifetime goals. Being over 65 now, I find that while I have accomplished much of what I have planned to do and hoped to attain so far, yet there is much more I look forward to fulfilling as I continue to follow my heart. I find that after fulfilling one set of potentials, a new goalpost appears to help me aim toward further growth and happiness. Life is never over until it is, allowing that from a spiritual point of view, death may be but a momentary transition to continuing one's spiritual journey. Until then, life here is full of constant new potentials.

My future based eulogy reaches back to me from its potential time of fulfillment. It reminds me to spend more time daily to explore and investigate my questions and to develop my capacity to be of greater service. I can read more, write more, contemplate more deeply, and open ever more to share with others pursuing similar life goals. I can also be more thankful for the experiences and relationships that have brought me this far, and for the path that wends forward from here bringing untold further possibilities.

YOUR TURN

Where are you today in terms of your life legacy, were you to pass beyond unexpectedly? As well, where might you hope to be in your life by the time of fulfilling your highest ambitions? Using the prompts in the Better Endings Story Seed at the end of this chapter you will be invited to compose two personal eulogies in the pages provided below, and/ or in your Better Endings Journal, from both now and from your future potential points of view. Remember to approach your ideal future eulogy as a *better endings* version that highlights the legacy you would ideally wish to leave for your loved ones.

What would you like others to understand about how you will have fulfilled your life's purpose by the time of your passing? What time capsule message to yourself from your self-realized future self can you embed in your projected eulogy, so you may strengthen your *better endings* ambitions going forward?

YOUR REFLECTIONS

Reflect in the pages provided below and/or in your Better Endings Journal about the sort of legacy you would hope to leave your loved ones at the time of your eventual departure.

How might the values and goals you have expressed in your *better endings* future eulogy represent a pathway forward for you to live your best life? What specific actions you can take now and in near the foreseeable future that could help you to actualize your goals?

CLOSING THOUGHTS

It does not matter what age you are now; your *better endings* eulogy can help you to claim or perhaps to reclaim your personal mission of life fulfillment. It is good if you find your eulogy as written from today or the near future to be a fine legacy to leave with your loved ones. Your current eulogy helps you recognize what you have already achieved and all you are thankful for.

Your *better endings* future eulogy includes your hopes and goals reaching forward from here. As a bucket list of more subtle desires, it reveals the *better endings* legacy you hope to leave behind: of core life lessons learned and the wisdom gained that you may happily pass along to others.

Your *better endings* eulogy is a time capsule from your future self.

Save it in the pages provided below and/or in your Better Endings Journal for a later time, when you can look back to see what milestones you have passed along the path to realize your truest ambitions.

Better Endings Story Seed

Your Better Endings Legacy

1. Compose a eulogy about yourself in the pages provided below, and/or in your Better Endings Journal from the point of view of the present. What would you like said about the life you have lived so far? Use the space below to list some facts you would like to include in your eulogy.

_____

_____

_____

_____

_____

2. Compose a second *better endings* eulogy as if it were written in the future by which time you will have fulfilled your deepest life goals. Use the space below to note ideas to include about your ideal future.

_____

_____

_____

_____

_____

My Reflections

Write about your lifetime legacy by which you would hope to be remembered. What have you achieved in your life so far? What have you yet to accomplish, to build and fulfill your greater legacy? What specific actions can you take now and in the near foreseeable future to help fulfill your *better endings* future legacy?

_____

_____

_____

_____

_____

_____

_____

_____

_____

_____

_____

_____

_____

_____

Conclusion

Your Best Is Yet to Come

I have selected the chapter topics of this book to introduce, and to engage you in applying for yourself, the creative principle of Better Endings. I hope you will continue to put this principle into practice long after you finish this book.

The stories we tell about ourselves—to ourselves as well as to others—give shape to the worlds we inhabit; past, present, and to come. Are we heroic in a world brimming with dynamic opportunity? Or meek in a world that hems in our desires? Have we overcome adversity, so we are able to face any coming challenge with confidence; or, are we haunted by shadowy ghosts from the past?

Are you happy?

I hope that the stories you tell in your *better endings* journaling with this book and well into your future will continue to illuminate your strengths and reveal what you are most grateful for as well as how you have met and learned from some of your most difficult challenges.

As the unique individual that you are, your story matters.

When I walked out of the theatre before King Kong could fall to his iconic death and wrote a re-visioned conclusion in which Kong survives, I stumbled into a goldmine of rich opportunity. I tapped into a vein of my own creative license—and yours! —to imagine and potentially improve upon not only fictional plotlines and historical memes but my own life story and potentially yours.

So live, and learn! Let that be your motto as you remain open to new opportunities that arise, both by your own choices and as surprising bends in the road. Socrates, whom I quoted earlier for his timeless message to each of us to "Know Thyself!" also had a powerful follow-up line. Plato taught his students that, "The unexamined life is not worth living."

The principle of Better Endings reveals the innate human capacity for creative re-visioning that anyone can use at any time. It can be used as a guiding light to illuminate the pitfalls in your path—past, present or future—so you can understand and improve upon any situation.

Humans (at least) are inherently a self-transcending species. We tell our stories and navigate through life day by day, aiming to do our best and potentially to better ourselves and our world for those we love. Sometimes we come up short of exercising our greatest potentials, or we stand back to let situations unfold in ways we might later come to regret. Your innate *better endings* lenses, like the rose-colored glasses I was given to wear on stage as an elder lady in a kindergarten play, are always available to you. They can help you to re-vision the past, to be more mindful in the present, and to foresee and better plan ahead with an eye to realizing your highest potentials.

I hope you will continue with your *better endings* journaling; that the self-discovery journaling prompts offered with this book are just a starter seed themselves for your continuing, lifelong practice of *better-endering*.

For me, as I have been living with the principle of Better Endings now for nearly a decade since beginning my blog at betterendingsnow. com, I have witnessed the potential effectiveness of drawing upon this principle firsthand, almost daily. I feel that my life has become a more flexible, self-fulfilling dream by which I can navigate memories as well as create brighter future prospects from the exciting, expansive viewpoint of Now.

Better Endings can become for you, too, a guiding principle; a way to follow your North Star forward, wherever it may bring you, and to listen to your Heart. You alone are responsible to recognize and actualize your deepest heart's desires; to discover and walk upon your own Higher Road.

May you discover and actualize your greatest life potentials, knowing this is an unending process of growth, flexibility, and reaching new horizons.

Whatever happens, may you find your Better Endings!

Better Endings Story Seed

Conclusion: Your Best Is Yet to Come!

1. Make a list of 3-5 key insights you have gained from applying the principle of Better Endings to your life story.

2. In the pages provided below and/or in your Better Endings Journal, write about the insights you have listed above. How will you take these insights forward?

My Reflections

Reflect in the pages provided below and/or in your Better Endings Journal about the value of creative re-visioning, or *better-endering,* as a tool you can draw upon when new challenges and choices arise. What are some additional situations from your life that would benefit from applying your *better endings* lens? Feel free to add more topics in your journal to write further *better endings* stories.